THE SWALLOW ANTHOLOGY
OF NEW AMERICAN POETS

THE SWALLOW ANTHOLOGY OF NEW AMERICAN POETS

EDITED BY DAVID YEZZI

FOREWORD BY J. D. McCLATCHY

SWALLOW PRESS
ATHENS, OHIO

Swallow Press / Ohio University Press, Athens, Ohio 45701
www.ohioswallow.com

© 2009 by Ohio University Press
All rights reserved

Printed in the United States of America
Swallow Press / Ohio University Press books are
printed on acid-free paper ⊚ ™

16 15 14 13 12 11 10   5 4 3 2

Library of Congress Cataloging-in-Publication Data

The Swallow anthology of new American poets / edited by David Yezzi ;
foreword by J.D. McClatchy.
       p. cm.
   ISBN 978-0-8040-1120-4 (alk. paper) — ISBN 978-0-8040-1121-1 (pbk. :
alk. paper)
    1. American poetry—21st century. I. Yezzi, David.
    PS617.S93 2009
    811'.608—dc22

                        2009023277

For Herbert Leibowitz

CONTENTS

FOREWORD

And here's one more way that poetry is like music. It's said that people's favorite tune is the one most popular when they first fell seriously in love—though probably everything surrounding such a moment remains memorable. It has to do with what the heart is paying rapt attention to. So too with poems. Our allegiances are formed by our first serious readings—the poems we get by heart, as it were. I don't mean childhood rhymes or classroom assignments. I mean those few poems that you parsed and plumbed, dazzled by their knowledge of your very soul. They are usually slightly elliptical: what we cannot grasp is the mystery that draws us in. For many, then, it was Emily Dickinson or Robert Frost who first revealed the stakes for which the game is played. But it could as easily have been Robert Herrick or Frank O'Hara.

The trouble is that those poems block out others. I had seen it happen. Friends with discerning taste and heightened intelligence would, when discussing the poetry of some master or peer, invariably return to the one early poem they had favored for decades. So I swore I would not let this happen to me. I swore—not just swore, *worked*—to keep myself open to new voices, different strategies. Even with those masters—Yeats, Stevens, Auden, Merrill, Hecht—whose work literally meant the world to me, I promised to keep shuffling the deck. But I didn't. I saw the same thing happen to myself that I had seen in other, better readers. I sealed the tomb and lit candles in front of the few shrines at which I had worshipped all along.

That is why I am especially grateful for the book you have in your hands now. When it came into mine, it revealed a whole new generation of exceptionally talented—*differently* talented—poets. As David Yezzi notes in his astute introduction, these thirty-five poets seem simply to have ignored the ideological wars that had raged in the magazines for half a century. He calls them "unified sensibilities," and that seems an apt term to describe a group of poets—I wouldn't say "a poetry" because these are a set of very individual writers—who haven't been blinded by fealties or hardened against traditional ways. It's probable that their teachers were embedded, on one side or the other, in those poetry wars, but these students—who undoubtedly paid attention and then read, under the sheets at night by flashlight, the books mocked in class—ignored those teachers who had insisted there is only one way to write a poem. Instead, they quickly got down to the task of writing, not of posing; of pursuing their poetic arguments through both what they had lived and what they had read (which is the best, or at least the clearest, part of life) rather than shrilly sounding one particular note or showing off their po-mo credentials.

If I were to generalize about the poets in this remarkable anthology, I would want to say something about the tone of this book. There is noticeably a common voice or approach. This is not a collection of vatic lyrics or dissociated rambles. The poems are often set at a middle distance, in a voice aware that it is speaking, pondering, puzzling, but alert as well to impulses that are unspoken or shocking. These are poets who have read, and who expect their readers also to have read. The poetry of the recent and distant past sometimes functions as a scaffolding but is rarely the excuse for a poem. These poets *use* their reading; they don't flaunt it. They like history, lore, *facts*, the kinds of details that annex new territory for the imagination to explore. And this gives their poems—of whatever length—a valuable amplitude. Facts, stubborn facts also prompt an informing irony and often a certain wryness. When these poets write of the personal life, they are never merely private. The ordinary pleasures and terrors of the domestic life reach out sensibly for moral dimensions and weight. The "personal" does not lie behind but upon a work of art: not Turner lashed to the mast in order to *experience* the storm at sea he will translate into a chaos of colors, but his fingerprint still visible today in the glob of pigment applied to make the sun that drove that storm aside.

Some of these poets would be called formalists, others not. But all of them are craftsmen rather than bards. They know how to knead and turn, glaze and fire. Their sense of poetic form is less the virtuosic display than the sign of care being taken to shape a thought or ease an emotion into unexpected consequences. They have tried, in other words, and with astonishing success, to avoid writing what Dr. Johnson called "tempo-rary poems." Above all, there is no sense here of improvisation, of things written about just because they were come upon. As Yvor Winters once wrote, "Poetry is the most difficult form of human utterance; we revise poems carefully in order to make them more nearly perfect. . . . We do not praise a violinist for playing as if he were improvising; we praise him for playing well. And when a man plays well or writes well, his audience must have intelligence, training, and patience in order to appreciate him. We do not understand difficult matters 'naturally.'"

As the editor of a journal, I read thousands of new poems every year. Most of them, as you might guess, are earnest or awkward, sleek or turgid. Invariably, though, from the miasma of smudged paper, the genuine *poem* leaps out, and asks for a true judgment. I have my own intuitive criteria, but as often as not I am happy to yield to those Elizabeth Bishop once recommended as the markers of a good poem: accuracy, spontaneity, and mystery. These are precisely the characteristics of the poems in this book. *Accuracy* is not literalism or pedantry; it is the ability to see and describe things as, at first glance or second thought, they truly are. *Spontaneity* is not improvisation or loafing; it is a fresh apprehension of the uneven textures of life. *Mystery* is not profundity or spirituality; it is the ability of a poem to clear space for what couldn't before have been anticipated, even by the poem itself—the passing thought or startling image that makes a thrilled reader stop and wonder. This is what good poems do. This is what David Yezzi's anthology does. You are holding now a whole new world of thought and feeling. Reading it will make it yours, will change your sense of what is possible and necessary. Plato, when he met Socrates, immediately burned his own poems. I am not suggesting you do that. I am suggesting you read these new poets, poets who question how we know what is familiar. You will not want to burn the poems you admire. You will want to add *these* to them.

J. D. McClatchy

INTRODUCTION

> I have many times asked myself, not without wonder,
> the source of a certain error which, since it is
> committed by all the old without exception, can be
> believed to be proper and natural to man: namely, that
> they nearly all praise the past and blame the present,
> revile our actions and behavior and everything which
> they themselves did not do when they were young,
> and affirm, too, that every good custom and way of
> life, every virtue and, in short, all things imaginable are
> always going from bad to worse.
>
> Baldesar Castiglione, *The Book of the Courtier*

If, as Castiglione believed, the old idealize the past, when spirits were lighter and customs more congenial, then the young tend not to regard it at all. And why should they? They are the exuberant custodians of the moment, free to establish the trends and conventions of their age in their own way and on their own terms. In fact, reverse Castiglione's formulation—replacing "old" with "young" and "past" with "present"—and one uncovers a reciprocal spirit in the young, which spurs them to praise the present and revile the past.

Here, then, are two extremes: call them Fogies and Badasses. Nostalgic for a time when the world conformed more readily to their ideas about everything from taxicabs to art, Fogies tend to see the world in a state of perpetual decline. Badasses, by contrast, worship the unique genius of "the now," as it springs forth fully formed from the head of the Zeitgeist. Fogies are crusty and set in their ways; Badasses, brash and eternally twentysomething. Unwieldy hybrids exist as well. There are premature Fogies—Young Turks clad in four-piece suits, who feel that little of value has emerged since the death of Queen Victoria—and balding Badasses, who are provisioning their RVs for their next trip to Burning Man. In the end, age is irrelevant; it's the no-holds-barred extremity that counts.

Critics love to break things into twos: Philip Rahv's redskins and pale-faces, Robert Lowell's raw and cooked (borrowed from the kitchen of Lévi-Strauss), Richard Wilbur's windows and doors, and Auden's Mabels and Alices. The age-old tension between classic and romantic figured by these pairs has, in certain respects, been a healthy one, and has led to some productive (and occasionally amusing) skirmishes. But when division leads to dogmatism there can be no forward movement. The old battle lines in poetry, between old and new, classic and romantic, formal and free, have become so entrenched that the young find little in the traditional to love and the old little in the new.

For the poets in this anthology, opposition may have outlived its usefulness. Here is a group of writers who have, perhaps for the first time since the modernist revolution of the early twentieth century, returned to a happy détente between warring camps. These poets do not constitute (thank God) a school. They are too diverse, too individual, too resistant to trends and fashions to be easily lumped together. They do, however, seem to me to possess (to adapt T. S. Eliot's phrase) a "unified sensibility," understanding the value of a tradition enlivened by innovation. (It is worth remembering that the experimental tradition has in many respects become as ossified and predictable as the conventional one.) This, I think, is a new—at least in our age—kind of poet, who, dissatisfied with the climate of extremes, has found a balance between innovation and received form, perceiving the terror beneath the classical and the unities girding romanticism. This new unified sensibility is no watered-down admixture, no pragmatic compromise worked out in departments of creative writing, but, rather, the vital spirit behind some of the most accomplished poetry being written by America's new poets.

Many people provided invaluable help in the compilation of this anthology. For their input and support, I would like to thank my wife, Sarah, Rick Barot, Priscilla Becker, Ben Downing, Dana Gioia, Ernest Hilbert, J. D. McClatchy, Michael Peich, Janet Polata, and C. Dale Young. Neil Azevedo, the former editor of Zoo Press, suggested I put this book together. Unfortunately, Zoo went under before the book could be realized. Enter David Sanders, who saw fit to revive the project with a number of alterations and an updated table of contents. David has carried on the fine tradition at Swallow Press with particular distinction. He is to my mind one of the very best editors of contemporary American poetry. I am deeply honored and grateful that David has allowed this anthology to fly Swallow's colors and carry its name.

David Yezzi

CRAIG ARNOLD

Craig Arnold was born near an air force base in 1967. His books of poetry are *Shells* (Yale University Press, 1999) and *Made Flesh* (Ausable/Copper Canyon, 2008). A past recipient of the Amy Lowell Poetry Travelling Scholarship, a National Endowment for the Arts fellowship, the Rome Prize, and a Fulbright, he was most recently awarded a United States–Japan Creative Artists residency. In late April 2009, Craig went missing while hiking on the small volcanic island of Kuchinoerabujima, Japan, and, as this volume was going to press, was presumed to have suffered a fatal fall.

The Singers

They are threatening to leave us   the nimble-throated singers
      the little murderers with the quick pulses
They perch at the ends of bare branches   their tails
      are ragged and pitiful   the long green
feathers are fallen out   They go on eating and eating
      last autumn's yellow melia-berries
They do not care that you approach   cold corpses
      rot in the grass   in the reeds
The gray-shouldered crows hobble about   the wren
      barely a mouthful   cocks her pert tail
and threatens to slaughter the white-footed cat in the bushes
      They do not understand that they are dying

They are threatening to leave us   how quickly we forget
      the way they taught us how to play our voices
opening soul to weightlessness   like the Spartan poet
      singing under the burden of his old bones
to the chorus-girls with their honey songs and their holy voices
      how he wished he could scoot like a kingfisher
lightly over the flower of the waves   who boasted
      I know the tunes of every bird but I Alkman
found my words and song in the tongue of the strident partridge
      Where will we find songs   when the sleek-headed
mallards are gone   who chase each other around the pond
      the reluctant duck and the lovesick drake
The way she turns her head to the side to scold him
      whack whack whack whack whack   the way her boyfriend
chases off his rival and then swims back   *reeb reeb*
      with feeble reassurances   the way
he sits on top of her   the way she flaps her wings
      to keep above water   the way they look

pleased with themselves   wagging their tails   smoothing
        each feather back in its right place

They are threatening to leave   but you may still catch them
        saying goodbye   stealthed in the cedar and cypress
at dawn   in the dark clarity between sleep and waking
        A run of five notes on a black flute
another   and another   buried deep in the mix
        how many melodies can the air hold
And what they sing   so lovely and so meaningless
        may urge itself upon you   with the ache
of something just beyond the point of being remembered
        the trace of a brave thought in the face of sadness

        For Boyce

Cedar Waxwings

    In photos they seem so dapper   their tails tipped yellow
            red-feathered wings   I think of them as yours

    You invited me over for lunch   you heated up some leftover
            chicken   stewed with walnut and pomegranate

    We'd been on our way to bed for weeks   we both knew it
            we felt it in our throats and in our lungs

    we tried to make the passage from table to bedroom seem
            less awkward   we spoke of Persephone

    we spoke of Inanna   stories that smell of dry-baked mud
            telling me stories was making your voice husky

Craig Arnold   3

and then a moment opened where I could touch your neck
        Later   when we had let go of each other

You speak of the land of the dead   I said   like one who's been there
        Yes you said   there was a boy who left you

hanging   as on a hook   you were neither here nor there
        everything blew through you   you noticed no one

not even your mother   now you were scaring me
        I could feel every inch of my nakedness

One winter morning you said   a flock of waxwings came
        and sat in the branches of the cedar tree

and stripped it clean of berries   for days you watched them flutter
        to and fro in the small square of the window

and then you felt your body gathering heft and substance
        the carpet pressing up against your bare feet

and you knew the sun was warm even through the cold glass
        and you put on socks   and came back to the living

I imagine their smooth colors   slate-gray and brown and yellow
        how the fan-branches would dip and sway

with the weight of so many   hanging upside down
        by their little feet   how they would tweak and whistle

passing the spicy dust-blue berries beak to beak
        like a bucket brigade   I am sorry if I left you

on a new hook   I am sick of hanging myself on memories
        If I had been less afraid   if I had paid

The Swallow Anthology of New American Poets

closer attention   you might be able now to remind me
          about those bright-winged birds   what power   what flair

what clarity or turbulence they have   to help the soul
          climb out of its own story   and look outside

          For Tzara

Incubus

The chain uncouples, and his jacket hangs
on the peg over hers, and he's inside.

She stalls in the kitchen, putting the kettle on,
buys herself a minute looking for two
matching cups for the lime-flower tea,
not really lime but linden, heart-shaped leaves
and sticky flowers that smell of antifreeze.
She talks a wall around her, twists the string
tighter around the teabag in her spoon.
But every conversation has to break
somewhere, and at the far end of the sofa
he sits, warming his hands around the cup
he hasn't tasted yet, and listens on
with such an exasperating show of patience
it's almost a relief to hear him ask it:
If you're not using your body right now
maybe you'd let me borrow it for a while?

It isn't what you're thinking. No, it's worse.

Why on earth did she find him so attractive
the first time she met him, propping the wall

at an awkward party, clearly trying to drink
himself into some sort of conversation?
Was it the dark uncomfortable reserve
she took upon herself to tease him out of,
asking, Are you a vampire? *That depends*,
he stammered, *are you a virgin?* No, not funny,
but why did she laugh at him? What made her think
he needed her, that she could teach him something?
Why did she let him believe that she was drunk
and needed a ride home? Why did she let him
take off her shirt, and fumble around a bit
on the spare futon, passing back and forth
the warm breath of a half-hearted kiss
they kept falling asleep in the middle of?
And when he asked her, why did she not object?
I'd like to try something. I need you to trust me.

Younger and given to daydreams, she imagined
trading bodies with someone, a best friend,
the boy she had a crush on. But the fact
was more fantastic, a fairy-tale adventure
where the wolf wins, and hides in the girl's red hood.
How it happens she doesn't really remember,
drifting off with a vague sense of being
drawn out through a single point of her skin
(a bedsheet threaded through a needle's eye)
and bundled into a body that must be his.
Sometimes she startles, as on the verge of sleep
you feel yourself fall backward over a brink,
and she snaps her eyelids open, to catch herself
slipping out of the bed, her legs swinging
over the edge, and feels the sudden sick

split-screen impression of being for a second
both she and her.

                What he does with her
while she's asleep, she never really knows,
flickers, only, conducted back in dreams:
Walking in neighborhoods she doesn't know
and wouldn't go to, overpasses, ragweed,
cars dry-docked on cinderblocks, wolf-whistles,
wanting to run away and yet her steps
planted sure and defiant. Performing tasks
too odd to recognize and too mundane
to have made up, like fixing a green salad
with the sunflower seeds and peppers that she hates,
pouring on twice the oil and vinegar
that she would like, and being unable to stop.
Her hands feel but are somehow not her own,
running over the racks of stacked fabric
in a clothing store, stroking the slick silk,
teased cotton and polar fleece, as if her fingers
each were a tongue tasting the knits and weaves.
Harmless enough.

                It's what she doesn't dream
that scares her, panic she can't account for, faces
familiar but not known, déjà vu
making a mess of her memory, coming to
with a fresh love-bite on her left breast
and the aftershock of granting another's flesh,
of having gripped, slipped in and fluttered tender,
mmm, unbraided, and spent the whole slow day
clutching her thighs to keep the chafe from fading,
and furious at being joyful, less
at the violation, less the danger, than the sense

he'd taken her enjoyment for his own.
That was the time before, the time she swore
would be the last—returning to her senses,
she'd grabbed his throat and hit him around the face
and threw him out, and sat there on the floor
shaking. She hadn't known how hard it was
to throw a punch without pulling it back.

Now, as they sit together on her couch
with the liquid cooling in the stained chipped cups
that would never match, no matter how hard
she stared at them, he seems the same as ever,
a quiet clumsy self-effacing ghost
with the gray-circled eyes that she once wanted
so badly to defy, that seemed to see her
seeing him—and she has to admit, she's missed him.
Why? She scrolls back through their conversations,
searching for any reason not to hate him.
She'd ask him, What's it like being a girl
when you're not a girl? His answers, when he gave them,
weren't helpful, so evasively poetic:
It's like a sponge somebody else is squeezing.
A radio tuned to all stations at once.
Like having skin that's softer but more thick.

Then she remembers the morning she awoke
with the smear of tears still raw across her cheeks
and the spent feeling of having cried herself
down to the bottom of something. Why was I crying?
she asked, and he looked back blankly, with that little
curve of a lip that served him for a smile.
Because I can't.
                    And that would be their secret.
The power to feel another appetite

pass through her, like a shudder, like a cold
lungful of oxygen or hot sweet smoke,
fill her and then be stilled. The freedom to fall
asleep behind the blinds of his dark body
and wake cleanly. And when she swings her legs
over the edge of the bed, to trust her feet
to hit the carpet, and know as not before
how she never quite trusted the floor
to be there, no, not since she was a girl
first learning to swim, hugging her skinny
breastless body close to the pool-gutter,
skirting along the dark and darker blue
of the bottom dropping out—
                          Now she can stand,
and take the cup out of his giving hand,
and feel what they have learned inside each other
fair and enough, and not without a kind
of satisfaction, that she can put her foot
down, clear to the bottom of desire,
and find that it can stop, and go no deeper.

Uncouplings

There is no I in *teamwork*
but there is a *two maker*

there is no I in *together*
but there is a *got three*
a *get to her*

the I in *relationship*
is the *heart I slip on*
a lithe prison

Craig Arnold   9

in all *communication*
we *count on a mimic*
(I am not uncomic)

our *listening skills*
are *silent killings*

there is no we in *marriage*
but a *grim area*

there is an I in *family*
also *my fail*

DAVID BARBER

David Barber was born in Los Angeles and educated at the University of California, Santa Cruz and Stanford University. He is the author of two collections of poems published by TriQuarterly Books/Northwestern University Press: *The Spirit Level* (1995, winner of the Terrence Des Prez Prize) and *Wonder Cabinet* (2006). He has received fellowship grants and awards from the National Endowment for the Arts, the Massachusetts Cultural Council, PEN/New England, and *Parnassus: Poetry in Review*. He is poetry editor of the *Atlantic Monthly*, where he has been on staff since 1994, and the Robert Frost Fellow in Poetry at Middlebury College. He lives outside Boston.

The Threshers

Observed too briskly, this could well be combat:
twin figures squared off with arms outstretched,
each shifting into the downstroke of a vehement blow

that means to relieve the rival of his head.
A pardonable error, for who of us knows a flail
when we see one, that odd implement come down to us

in the garb of a verb? It looks like a cross
between a hockey stick and a carpenter's square,
but swung just so, it served famously for those who beat

wheat from chaff, as the saying goes—though if accuracy
is what we crave, it's best to speak of flogging out
kernel and seed from husks and stems. That's what's meant

at the root by *threshing*, and that's what the woodcut
is illustrating, shrunk to the size of a postage stamp
beside the citation in my antiquated unabridged.

So they do not intend to brain each other, after all,
those foursquare characters, the threshers. They are toiling
in unison, flailing a sketchy mound of grain

strewn across the entrance of a rustic structure
(the threshold!), ushering in a representative autumn
in the early 19th century. No doubt they timed their strokes

with seasoned aplomb, wise to the other's arc and swath.
A crackerjack duo must have struck a clockwork groove.
Securely bucolic, their industry cannot entirely escape

an undercurrent of ruthlessness: the grip on the shaft
says the lash is the gist. The tendentious English tongue
saw to it this strain assumed the upper hand

when the vowel began to shift—thus, whosoever will *thrash*
calls up the ghost of the brute force such men mustered
to whip ripe wheat, to drub the summer crop.

Noah Webster's myrmidons counsel us that it's proper
either way, but surely they're behind the curve.
Anyone beset with garden-variety night sweats can thrash,

but threshers are an utterly uprooted breed, dumbstruck,
their exertions embalmed in figures of speech.
It's like getting a postcard from a suburb of Babel,

having them materialize like this, throwbacks
to the grit-caked literal instance underwriting the idiom,
the palpable heft and sinew beneath what learned heads

of the day were wont to call "the dress of thought."
So much for sweeping language, then: let me stress
their innate stick-to-itiveness, the sweat of their brow,

their exacting stamina that might still be aptly emulated
by all who hope to lay to rest appearances of conflict
by mulling it over, working it through, thrashing it out.

Matchbook Hymn

Ivy, for scaling.
Iceplant, for creeping.

Green shields, green spears.
A family lies sleeping.

New runners, fresh shoots.
Ivy, for screening.
Downslope a man kneels.
Iceplant, for hedging.

Blast-furnace summers.
Tinderbox evenings.
Ivy, for braiding.
Iceplant, for weaving.

Hazy sun, sooty sky.
What's the radio saying?
Ivy and iceplant.
A woman keeps pacing.

A house on a hillside.
Dry annuals flaring.
Ivy, for grasping.
Iceplant, for reaching.

The Lather

On the tin stowed under the upstairs sink
The mule team circulates in silhouette:
Yeoman hand-scrub of workingmen and sons
Going back to before his father was born.

And so he pictures vast bleached dunes
Shimmering to the vanishing point,
The chalky powder heaped in mounds
And hauled to the city by wagon train

To meet demand, a grand procession.
So let tar bleed from telephone poles,
Let engine blocks ooze rainbow slicks
And bike chains jam with caked-up gunk—

He's heard his father say one scoop will cut
Through any crap, no matter what,
Just work the lather good, keep at it.
He's fallen into rhythm now, a little remote,

A little dreamy: the team marches round
The tin like ants, his wrists turn and turn
In a reaming motion, and his head spins
To think of all the pitch-black hands

Squelching away at this dinner hour,
Filling washbasins with oily rivers.
And now his suds froth even darker.
His skin's on fire. He feels certain

The storied mines can't last forever:
The dunes will dwindle into moon dust,
The mules will litter the desert floor
With hollow skulls. He knows in his bones

He's turning into the kind of upstart
Who never misses a chance to flout
A father's orders about what not to touch
Or take apart. In the fogging mirror

He sees himself far older, doubled over
Fiendish smears that won't rinse out
(Some industrial taint? Indelible ink?)
Faithfully, furiously, though he scours.

David Barber

A Colonial Epitaph Annotated

Here lies as silent clay
Miss Arabella Young
Who on the 21st of May, 1771
Began to hold her tongue

Here rests as circumspect dust
A maid who spoke her mind
Without the ghost of a blush
Or a nod to her prim kind.

Here silt her tart remarks
And her spirited retorts,
Her mordant takes on politics
And the sermon's finer points.

Here chafes in stony hush
An erstwhile spitfire.
Finally they could rest in peace,
The fools she wouldn't suffer!

Here in her boneyard bower
Look sharp for the shards of a quip.
The lady was no flower.
She'd cut you to the quick.

Here beneath this slate
You can sense her mute dismay,
Who was the soul of wit
And revelled in repartee.

Here lies as silent clay
Miss Arabella Young.

Be that as it may,
Here's to the sting in her tongue.

Eulogy for an Anchorite

Brother Adam, devout bee breeder,
Today the paper ran your obit.
A brisk write-up, yet how it brims
With the lambent amber of your bliss.
Your abiding faith in the honeybee
Imbued your days with abounding grace.

"Brother Adam, Benedictine monk,
Transformed beekeeping, at 98 . . ."
I adore that squib. I laud your slant
On beatitude and humble soulcraft.
I love the fact your name was gold
In apiaries around the globe.

Brother Adam, from Buckfast Abbey
In Britain's toe, you would abscond
(Often on foot, or astride a donkey)
To Araby and the Holy Land,
There to bushwhack for robust strains
To husband in your cloistered hives.

At ninety, admirable Brother Adam,
You bobbed to the top of Kilimanjaro
Strapped to the back of a kindred spirit
In pursuit of the burly Monticola.
Brother Adam, that took some aplomb.
It buoys me simply to think of it.

O Brother Adam, if I may be so bold,
You must have harbored no higher rapture
Than when a swarm's harmonious hubbub
Swelled into a thrumming rumble.
The heather bloomed, the nectar flowed:
What choir ever soared any sweeter?

You're the stuff of fable, Brother Adam.
Your little sisters, how they labor!
We sybarites owe you a lasting debt.
To spurn the temptations of the flesh
Only to leave the world more toothsome—
Now, there's a parable to savor.

Brother Adam, redoubtable beekeeper,
You belong on the glazed pane of a chapel
Bedecked in your habit and your veil
Hard by the other miracle workers.
There hovers about you a burnished aura
Befitting a harbinger of ambrosia.

Brother Adam, Brother Adam,
When it comes to combs, you split the atom.
Every kingdom has its keys.
They've baptized your hybrids "superbees."
The heartbreaking millennium runs down,
But Brother Adam, your renown's a balm.

Brother Adam, I'm no believer.
When I'm not bedeviled, I'm beleaguered.
But consider your bees, in clover season—
Didn't they seem possessed by demons?

Let me grapple, let me fumble.
I may yet become your true disciple.

Wallenda Sutra

Life's on the wire;
The rest is waiting. I know
I'm alive when I

Hear no one breathing.
On the wire I'm living:
The wire is where

I'm sure where I stand
In the great chain of being.
The rest is dead air;

The rest is waiting.
When I'm out on the wire,
Beyond all wanting,

It's clear that the rest
Of my life is sleepwalking.
Stadiums, gorges,

Standing room only—
That's me in the viewfinder,
Making my living.

Life's on the wire,
Where everything's trembling;
The rest is nothing

David Barber

But worry and care.
On the wire I'm at one
With all my past lives,

Treading the fine line
Between the worms and the stars.
The rest is stalling;

The rest is chafing.
Wherever there's wires, that's
Where I'll be waiting.

RICK BAROT

Photo by David Borrelli

Rick Barot was born in 1969 in the Philippines and grew up in the San Francisco Bay Area. His books of poetry are *The Darker Fall* (2002), which won the Kathryn A. Morton Prize in Poetry, and *Want* (2008), both published by Sarabande Books. He has received fellowships from the National Endowment for the Arts and Stanford University, where he was a Wallace Stegner Fellow and a Jones Lecturer. He lives in Tacoma, Washington, and teaches at Pacific Lutheran University and in the Program for Writers at Warren Wilson College.

Study

It has taken its time to come to it, the tree nearly
clean of leaves. With even a querulous wind,

something on it flurries into wing. How it must
happen: first, the leaves' release, then the limbs'

paralysis, frost on the wizened trunk like pollen.
Then each thing keeping to itself. The house

an entire thought to itself. This morning I saw her
take a coffee can of seed to the feeder, so cold

that her breath seemed a ghost-face always
in front of her. In brown explosive handfuls

the birds disbanded. Her work took long minutes.
Step and step, the feeder's lid removed, the can

aimed into it, then the steps back, the birds back,
the screen door slightly open, a dumb mouth.

In the afternoon, in the day's one warm hour,
he was up on a ladder taking down storm windows,

hosing them down, the paste-white sky reflected
when he tipped each wet square a certain way.

The tufts of one glove waved in his back pocket.
The other lay on the grass. It was there long enough

for me to see their room darkened, the clothes
heaped, the white alp of a foot underneath a sheet.

Nearing Rome

So much open emotion that
our disbelief seemed beside the point—
"You think I want your irony,"
he said to her.
                    The train shrieked
its way out of a curve. Outside, wheat
looked like the tousled hair
of someone's childhood.
                    And maybe,
as in some novel which has it in mind
to curdle its characters'
good natures in the end, we would all
have to be that plaintive
and ridiculous—
                    the old man interminably
peeling a boiled egg; the beautiful
dark woman reading Simenon in Spanish;
even the kid whose teeth were dirty
with purple crayon.
                    And you, who hadn't
looked up in hours, even when I said
that the air coming in smelled
of sawdust, and the backyard activity
we sometimes passed—a woman hanging up
laundry, a boy spraying grain
to chickens—
                    just a quaint dying memory
of an old order.

Rick Barot

At Point Reyes

I was old. I could see this in the will
of the ocean moving in, the lavish force.

Among the seaweed were finger bones
of driftwood, some feathers, flame-blue

and teeth-white. The water was the same
as I had known it: light green within

the thinning wall of its arc, the horizon
behind it. I felt separate but unhurt,

the smallest trapeze swinging on inside
my chest. From the pieces eroded

to chalk by the sand, I had to remember
what it meant to have ruined something,

bottle after bottle cracking against rocks.
Dead things, souring in the salt air:

this was my exhaustion. The iceplants
glistened plastic pink, the poppies furled

into bullets. I started to get cold, cold
as a leaf on someone's palm. A line of

breath followed everything that I said
to myself. Somewhere in the cordgrass

I found a pair of glasses, an insect-leg
tangle of rusted wires. The sunset began

to answer the things I had my heart on:
the snowglobe city, its durable lights;

the view from a window down to wet cars,
each roof a nail painted in black polish.

Reading Plato

I think about the mornings it saved me
to look at the hearts penknifed on the windows
of the bus, or at the initials scratched

into the plastic partition, in front of which
a cabbie went on about bread his father
would make, so hard you broke teeth on it,

or told one more story about the plumbing
in New Delhi buildings, villages to each floor,
his whole childhood in a building, nothing to

love but how much now he missed it, even
the noises and stinks he missed, the avenue
suddenly clear in front of us, the sky ahead

opaquely clean as a bottle's bottom, each heart
and name a kind of ditty of hopefulness
because there was one *you* or another I was

leaving or going to, so many stalls of flowers
and fruit going past, figures earnest with
destination, even the city itself a heart,

so that when sidewalks quaked from trains
underneath, it seemed something to love,
like a harbor boat's call at dawn or the face

reflected on a coffee machine's chrome side,
the pencil's curled shavings a litter
of questions on the floor, the floor's square

of afternoon light another page I couldn't know
myself by, as now, when Socrates describes
the lover's wings spreading through the soul

like flames on a horizon, it isn't so much light
I think about, but the back's skin cracking
to let each wing's nub break through,

the surprise of the first pain and the eventual
lightening, the blood on the feathers drying
as you begin to sense the use for them.

Bonnard's Garden

As in an illuminated page, whose busy edges
have taken over. As in jasmine starred
onto the vine-dense walls, stands of phlox,
and oranges, the flesh of each chilled turgid.

By herself the sleepwalking girl arranged
them: the paper airplanes now wrecked
on the vines, sodden, crumpled into blooms
which are mistaken all morning for blooms.

The paint curls out of the tubes like ointments.
In his first looking there is too much hurry.
Dandelions, irises smelling of candles.
Two clouds like legs on the bathwater sky.

Drawn out of the background green, getting
the light before everything else, the almond

tree comes forward in a white cumulus,
as though the spring had not allowed leaves.

Last night she asked what temperature arctic
water could be that beings remained in it.
Then the question brought to the blood
inside her cat, the pillow of heat on a chair.

His glimpse smudged. As in: it's about time
I made you dizzy. Here are pink grasses,
shrubs incandesced to lace, tapestry
slopes absorbing figures and birds and deer.

Nothing is lean. The lilacs have prospered
into bundles, the tulips fattened hearts.
Pelts of nasturtiums, the thicket the color of
pigeon: gray netted over the blueberry lodes.

Then the girl's scream, her finger stirring
the emerald tadpole-water, the sound
breaking into his glimpse for an instant
then subsiding to become a part of the picture.

Not the icy killing water. But the lives there,
persisting aloft. Like the wasps held in
by a shut flower at dusk, by morning released,
dusty as miners, into the restored volumes.

The Horses

The primary red striped onto the black, the dye
            spotting the mirror and sink with
a kind of gore, a sulfur that is in the air for days:
            you are twenty-two and this means

even folly has its own exacting nature. The hair
                turned red, as easily as last month's
blue; the puggish, miniature barbell pierced into
                a nipple. At the club I watch you on top

of the speaker, tearing the shirt your brother gave
                you, the music a murderous brightness
in the black room. Now you want it all off, down
                to clear scalp. Your head in foam,

you ask me to do the places you can't properly
                reach: the neck's mossy hairs, the back's
escarpment, an edge of bone the razor nicks
                to small blood, tasting like peppermint

and metal on my tongue. In the used bookstore
                this afternoon, in the old master's book of
drawings, pencil sketches of the heads of horses,
                whose long nostrils had been slit open

as custom demanded. The Icelanders, Mongols,
                and Italians finding a measurable
efficiency in what they could see: the horses, even
                in their speed, as though not breathing.

Iowa

It is something to be thus saved,
                a point on which the landscape
comes to a deep rest.

The ore of a death held
                frozen, there in the gull so far
inland, embedded in the ice

at the river's edge. Its bulk
          in the thick gloss is darker
than the ice, shoe-shaped,

only the spoon-curved head
          telling you what it is, one eye
open though no longer sustaining.

The feet are ribbed, like sails
          tight on a mast. And a thing,
you remember, obliges by lying

down, its back to sky. How long
          it has been like this, this little
a question to the world.

How small of a happening, though
          it happened because
there is witness of it. The width

of water utterly silent,
          the distance a pencil-smudge
of Chinese hills. First its fall,

then immersion, every air discovered
          out of each quill,
its feathers matted with grit.

The day is a white octave, breathing
          its snow, and the bird
delicate, like a bone inside the ear.

Priscilla Becker's first book of poems, *Internal West*, won the *Paris Review* book prize. Her poems have appeared in *Fence*, *Open City*, the *Paris Review*, *Small Spiral Notebook*, *Boston Review*, *Raritan*, *American Poetry Review*, *Passages North*, and *Verse*; her music reviews in the *Nation* and *Filter*; her book reviews in the *New York Sun*; and her essays in *Cabinet* and *Open City*. Her essays have also been anthologized by Soft Skull Press, Anchor Books, and Sarabande. Her second book, *Stories That Listen*, will be published by Four Way Books. She teaches poetry at Pratt Institute, at Columbia University, and in her Brooklyn apartment.

Last in Water Series

When it is time, I will choose
the most beautiful river.
I compare swatches cut
from maps, samples drawn
from the world's waters.

It's been a while since
I was surrounded in element,
some time since
the blue mothering.

I am aware of the marble-
patterned floor—dizzying
but not warm.

It is a mutual need,
and even when I am doing
the most obscure thing,
I sense the water
moving toward me.

I smell the river's brine
as though it's the water
            inside me.

I'd like for my river
to be visited infrequently,
for the sediment to be high.

The sound it will make,
a calling.

Priscilla Becker

Not my name
but my name
before there was speech.

New Desert

There is a new desert
where the old one was—
new bugs, a black
kind of sand

Recently here there was
a water source,
there was sun
but it did not scorch

Not all deserts
are the same:
when I say *tree*
you ask which one,
desert and everybody
pictures the same one

Even were I to
give it a name—
new desert, blue
desert, black
desert, desert
that dried up
the previous one—
you'd see expanse
of sand, no people,
a camel every now

and then, a caravan,
pale sky that meets
the sand

But this one has a rift
in it, a place where
the old sand ends.
Walk to its edge,
look down in it,
and from nothing,
unblinking, new sand

It is a new desert
for a little while—sand
unused to the burning sun,
disquieted by the expanse
of itself, sand
made sleepy by the desert's
shallow pulse

The young desert
does not know
what it will become

Neglect

The life that was
waiting for me is
gone. It was
there so long I'd
thought it was
part of me.

It used to hover
at the skin of me
or farther off
like a boy
I once kept
not too far,
close

enough to be
a motion I thought
my own.

It didn't happen
suddenly
or in dark.
In truth it went
patiently
like someone
packing from a list,
planning to
go thoroughly

In truth it went
slow.

I think of it now
but without it
it's like a privacy
emptied-out, a thought
closed.

It's not that: I've been
left before. It's like
when I was young,

what I thought
music was.

Once it loved nothing
but to wait for me

and I thought it
somewhere I could go.
Thought I could walk
into it when I was
done, like

entering a building
whose objects come
from home,
just enough
like my life that I'd
go, and at the back
not a light but
a source.

In a certain way,
nothing's much
changed. It's like
not knowing to count
and then counting
to one.

Monarch

Your rule has made an August
of October and I am lazy

in my domicile as maple leaves
turn half yellow and forget
the ailing spectrum.

This season there are many
kings; I've made a shrine
to orange things, a coterie
of me and three domestic-
leaning cats whose naps fulfill
a mossy genuflection brought on
by molding walls, delays
in evolution.

I thought I saw you drinking from
a branch between the pickets
of a fence, and in two gestures
you define first aviation,
then verticality. And as I wait

for long-diverted patterns, triumphal
browns, the cat's serene totem
of itself says there's a lineage
denied me. Still I would like to rule
a small bud too, but I have neither
your erect and glassy wings nor
did I come from emerald shroud:
I drink the milk of thistle, preferring
it to natural motherings.

Seasonal Poem

Snow would be the right weather
for today. Whiteness indicating

things that don't exist. And a numbness
and a blanketing to recollect mother

Its second stage is frozenness, and though I long
for its touch across my face, its coldness
settling, what seems to happen
quicker than it should is the snow's
paralysis. How willing it is
to take on other substances. How I used to run
to it barefoot before I thought
of my own comfort.

But the fall for which we've wished
the year is reticent; it hates its unreal
status, its intermittentness.

I could take a job—I've been thinking
about my purposes—collecting ice
for the eyes of the princess

Snowdonia

Not that the hair is blond,
but that it is not brown.
My mistake.

Not even once to settle
curiosity, or hiding on the legs
beneath my clothes.

The same way a violet
is not really blue and so
can live in two fields at once.

Priscilla Becker   37

Or more.
Now I think I understand
the litany of jokes—

a visible absence
positioned on my head,
a station in the arc

of vanishing.
Not hard then to imagine
dropping one more notch below

to white, which means a hollow
follicle, a life of exhausting
chameleonism.

See. We're happy again.

White Tone

I think I prefer now being unloved
and listening for my footsteps in the dark.

There was a tree in the yard—
not anymore—
whose crooked branch I'd watch.

I held a ceremony in which I married
my black dog.

There is a certain smell
that overtakes me, for instance
once, in a button shop.

And then I came to disregard.

Also a kind of nakedness
that has to do with words.

I made a list
of things I'd like. I tied
a string. The sound as when your foot
breaks through the snow,
that sound was in the house.

Photo by Johnathon Williams

Geoffrey Brock, born in Atlanta in 1964, is the author of *Weighing Light*, winner of the New Criterion Poetry Prize (Ivan R. Dee, 2005), and the translator of several books from the Italian, including Cesare Pavese's *Disaffections* (Copper Canyon, 2002), Umberto Eco's *The Mysterious Flame of Queen Loana* (Harcourt, 2005), and Carlo Collodi's *Pinocchio* (New York Review Books, 2009). He has been a Stegner Fellow, a National Endowment for the Arts Fellow, and a Guggenheim Fellow, and he now teaches creative writing and translation at the University of Arkansas in Fayetteville.

And Day Brought Back My Night

It was so simple: you came back to me
And I was happy. Nothing seemed to matter
But that. That you had gone away from me
And lived for days with him—it didn't matter.
That I had been left to care for our old dog
And house alone—couldn't have mattered less!
On all this, you and I and our happy dog
Agreed. We slept. The world was worriless.

I woke in the morning, brimming with old joys
Till the fact-checker showed up, late, for work
And started in: *Item: it's years, not days.*
Item: you had no dog. Item: she isn't back,
In fact, she just remarried. And oh yes, item: you
Left her, remember? I did? I did. (I do.)

The Beautiful Animal

By the time I recalled
that it's also terrifying,
we'd gone too far into

the charmed woods
to return. It was then
the beautiful animal

appeared in our path:
ribs jutting, moon-fed
eyes moving from me

to you and back. If we
show none of the fear,
it may tire of waiting

for the triggering flight,
it may ask only to lie
between us and sleep,

fur warm on our skin,
breath sweet on our necks
as it dreams of slaughter,

as we dream alternately
of feeding and taming it
and of being the first

to run. The woods close
tight around us, lying
nested here like spoons

in a drawer of knives,
to see who wakes first,
and from which dream.

Her Voice When She Is Feeling Weak

Her voice when she is feeling weak creates
a double pull in me, as a phone can
when it rings and rings and rings and no one else

will answer it, and the machine that states
I'm not here right now is broken again,
and all day I've expected these two calls:

one from the creditor who likes to foretell
(with the shrill ardor of a true believer)
the grim details of my financial fate;

the other from a room in some hotel,
and all I want is to reach for the receiver
and hear her say she's fine and won't be late.

The Last Dinner Party

For Kim Garcia

The usual sounds: forks on plates, and voices,
and the easy laughter of friends together—and I,

too, am laughing, and happy, and a little drunk.
Then I walk down the hall and close the door,

muting the laughter. I lean toward the mirror
and see myself three times: the bloated visage

that grows from my neck, and the eyeless twin
that floats in the jar of each pupil. When I return

to the table of my friends, I bring the silence back.
It sits with me until Kim says something funny

and I can't help laughing again, and then David
says something even funnier, and then Frank,

and we're on some kind of roll, gathering threads
from earlier conversations and weaving them in,

weaving the whole evening into one tight fabric
that we wrap around ourselves like a shared belief,

Geoffrey Brock

and for a few graceful moments we are gaining on time,
all of us laughing and blinking tears from our eyes.

The Starvers

Two bull elk lay dead in the snow, antlers
locked. It was October, rutting season,

the Canadian hills were splotched like the sky
with white, and you stood there beside me,

repulsed by the carcasses, by the way
their elk eyes stared dully toward the earth,

the glaze of their astonishment fading.
Just like men, you said, turning

to walk back to the truck, putting that distance
between us. I stayed a while, and winters came,

and summers. I don't think of you often.
But when the weather's right, I can see the bulls

sinking down together, wet nostrils flaring,
to starve. The does wandering away.

The sky like this one, lurid blue and tilted sharply,
and that single shapely cloud spilling off.

Mezzo Cammin

Today, as I jogged down the center line
of a closed-off, rain-glossed road, lost in a rhythm,
the memory of a boy returned: fifteen

or so, barefoot in faded cut-off jeans,
sprinting past neighbors' houses, tears drifting
into his ears, heart yanking at its seams—

he hoped they'd rip and didn't slow at all
for more than a mile. After crossing Mission,
the boy collapsed beneath an oak, his whole

body one cramp. (But later the secret smile,
imagining Guinness there—the clock-men stunned!)
Twenty years gone, that race so vivid still,

yet I can't for the life of me recall the gun:
who was it, or what, that made me start to run?

Homeland Security: 2006

The four a.m. cries
of my son worm
through the double
foam of earplugs

and diazepam.
The smoke alarm's
green eye glows.
Beneath the cries,

the squirm and bristle
of the night's catch
of fiddlebacks
on the glue-traps

guarding our bed.
Necrotic music.

Scored in my head.
And all night columns

of ants have tramped
through the ruins
of my sleep, bearing
the fipronil

I left for them
home to their queen.
Patriot ants.
Out of republics

endlessly perishing.
If I can hold
out long enough,
maybe my wife

will go. If she
waits long enough,
maybe he'll go back
down on his own.

The Nights

The screamer sleeps, inside.
The desert's wide awake:
the mouse, the rattlesnake.
I've come out here to hide,

behind our house, below
the riddled sky, afraid

of what our bodies made.
To the south: Mexico . . .

These are the nights men run.
Guaymas before midday,
a beach-town life . . . I play
it out. Such things are done.

The Rincons seep like a stain
into the paling east.
The borders are policed.
The wail, nearby, of a train.

One Morning

The boy is wide awake:
he climbs into our bed
and clambers toward my head,
wielding a yellow rake.

Combing my hair, the boy
giggles with every stroke.
His is a simple joke:
he knows his plastic toy

is not a comb, my hair
is not disheveled sand,
and yet his furrowed mind
has seen a likeness there—

delight grows from small seeds.
And for now I won't worry

Geoffrey Brock

what else might, as we hurry
toward what the future breeds.

Diretto

Forgive my scrawl: I'm writing this in the near dark
    So as not to wake you. I'm amazed you're sleeping;
I can't. Whenever we grind into some rural station,
    I wait for your eyes to tighten or to snap

Open with fright, with that *oh-shit-what's-happening* look
    That sometimes comes to them on sudden waking,
Even at home—if a cat, say, jumps from the bed,
    Tamping the floor, or the heater stutters on.

Your eyes stay shut but not still, moving beneath their lids
    To a rhythm as far beyond me as the landscapes
Of shadow that unreel themselves on the far side
    Of this drawn vinyl shade . . . We're slowing, again,

To a stop. Someone's shuffling off, dragging a bag—
    If you hear that, you hear it as something else,
And if you feel our gentle waking from inertia
    As the train moves again, you feel it elsewhere.

Someone's walking toward us—they try our door: it's locked.
    Selfish, I know, but I don't want to share
The sight of you asleep. In the next compartment a suitcase
    Chunks on the rack, then a sound like a struck match—

And I imagine cities blazing in your sleep.
    I want to ask what country you're awake in,

What haunts you in that place, what ecstasies arouse you . . .
    Everything wants to dream itself into something

Larger tonight: the train, this warm compartment, the seen
    And unseen. Let's say they're just themselves. That you
Are here with me. And that these words are just a transcript
    Of this, the night of your heroic sleep.

Photo by Ellen Frieder

Daniel Brown was born in New York City in 1950. His book of poetry, *Taking the Occasion* (Ivan R. Dee), won the 2008 New Criterion Poetry Prize. His poems and criticism have appeared in *Poetry*, the *New Criterion*, *Partisan Review*, *Harvard Review*, and other journals, as well as in a number of anthologies, including *The Pushcart Prize XI*, *Poetry 180*, and *Fathers*. His *Why Bach?* (Crosstown Books), an online appreciation of Bach's music, is available at WhyBach.com. He works at IBM, and lives in Baldwin, New York.

Missing It

The thing about the old one about
The tree in the forest and nobody's around
And how it falls maybe with a sound,
Maybe not, is you throw the part out
About what there isn't or there is,
And the part of it that haunts is still there.
Still there in that the happening, the clear
Crashing there, still encompasses
Everyone condemned to missing it
By being out of the immediate
Vicinity. Out of it the way
You're out of all vicinities but one
All the time—excepting when you've gone
Out of all vicinities to stay.

The Birth of God

It happened near Lascaux
Millions of dawns ago.
For dawn it was,
Infusing radiance
And cuing avians
The way it does,

That saw the two of them
(Odds are a her and him,
Though maybe not)
Emerging from the mouth
Of a cave a couple south
Of the one that's got

All that painted fauna
All but snorting on a
Wall. That is
To say, from the mouth of a cave
Unconsecrated save
By the sighs and cries

Of the night just past. The pair
Has borne the bliss they share
Out into the bright.
Where silently they stand
Thanking, hand in hand
Before the light.

Their gratitude is truly
New beneath the duly
Erupting sun.
A gratitude that so
Wants a place to go
It authors one.

My Own Traces

Dishes sinked, food stowed—
Time for me to hit the road.
A yank at the cord of what
I'd call the kitchen light if this
Nook were more of an excuse
For calling it that.

Whereupon my making for
The freedom of the front door,

In the course of which is when
The awful certainty of my
Never sealing up the rye
Bread steals in.

Nothing but to turn around,
Back-track to where I find
Myself reentering
The province of the kitchenette,
Only to confront the sight
Of the light-cord aswing.

Not the first case of my
Own traces taking me
Completely by surprise.
Moving me to mutter "So
I *do* exist"—much as though
I'd had it otherwise.

When It Happened

Am I unusual in remembering
Exactly when? I was verging on thirteen
When a story in a *Mad* magazine
Brought me to a picture of a string-
Bikinied cutie standing on a dock.
A panel in a comic, nothing more,
Yet all it took to get me reaching for
A pencil with intent to have a look
Beneath those bits she wore. I saw things through
By blacking in two nipples and a hole
(My notion of it being spherical).

Regarded what I'd rendered—only to
Recoil from it wondering. As though
The renderer was one I didn't know.

Though Angelless

> I once glanced up at a tree and found it full of angels singing
> praises to God.
>
> *Blake*

If I'm to take this visionary quote
As something of a challenge (not a bad
Way of taking everything he wrote)
It isn't one I'd be exactly glad
To tackle. *Angels* thronged those wild eyes!
The realist in me would settle for
The gleam (to name a consolation prize)
That Wordsworth was at pains to say he saw
In nature (as a kid at least), but this,
If it ever lent its lucence to my view,
Has been long since retired to the shelf.
Which doesn't mean a tree, though angelless,
Won't move me now and then to loose a few
Notes of praise from the old throat myself.

Prayer

Repeatedly
A new house
Larger than
The previous—

In each case
The previous

Persisting as
A part of us—

This growth as
Of the nautilus
May our selves
Suffer us.

Something Like That

You know how in Spanish they put
An -ita on things? So this girl
Mildred, this Puerto Rican girl
Where I work, pretty girl—so I get
To thinking that a funny thing about
Her name is that it's one thing that now
That you think of it it isn't clear how
To ita-ize.
                    I'd come right out
And ask her how, but figure it's a bit
Safer to let the questioning begin
With a little in the way of easing in.
As in it is Spanish isn't it
Where they do that, and are we talking small
Things specifically or is it more
Like anything you have affection for
(As if I didn't know already)—all
Of which preliminary inquiries
Get me to the one I'm getting at:
Did they ever call her something like that
When she was a kid?
                    Only lowered eyes.
Then, like something she's confessing to,

That her father did. And would she mind my
Asking what it was? No reply,
So I try a little prompting with a few
Possibilities. Not to press her,
But I've got to know how that would go:
Mildrita? "No." Mildredita? "No."
Mildredecita? "No!" Then . . . "Princesa."

"Why Do I Exist?"

Answer it? Nobody can
(To go by the hordes that haven't yet).
But as for having the question down,
You know you're really asking it
When it isn't merely answerless
But answerless in the strongest sense:
Answerless in being less
A question than an utterance.

A Math Grad

Math's a matter some make
More of than the norm. I'm
Thinking of a math grad
I shared a loft with for a time.
Who a while back had had a break-
Down, he once confessed from bed

To bed. Nothing he thought about
A lot. . . . He pauses. Then goes on
To speak, sane-seemingly enough,

Of a funny class of functions. One
Whose characteristic graph starts out
With the usual smooth take-off,

Somewhere along the line goes
Into a beauty of a loop-
De-loop for whatever reason, then
Picks its rising right up
Where it left off, and never does
Anything like that again.

On Being Asked by Our Receptionist if I Liked the Flowers

"What flowers?" I said. "These flowers," she said,
Gesturing leftward with her head,
And there it was: a vase of flowers
That hadn't graced that fort of hers
The day before. Did I say a vase?
All of an urn is what it was:
Capacious home to a bursting sun
Of thirty lilies if to one.
A splendor I'd have seen for sure,
If less employed in seeing her.

On Brooklyn Heights

Along their elevated edge (in case
You didn't know, a heights they really are)
A mayor got to feeling generous
And went and did (thank God) the obvious;

Which is to say installed a walkway there
(Or promenade, to use the moniker

The locals use). A venue, to be sure,
For devotees of harbor-breeze and sun,
But even more a place one visits for
The *vista* it affords the visitor:
That bridge-with-city-scape of such renown
(Myself, I'd settle for the bridge alone).

A sight my vision was at feed upon
One morning, when there passed in front of me
A father with a baby fastened on—
All right, so hung against—his chest in one
Of those . . . those what exactly? Seems that I
Should know, though there's the fact that I'm a guy

Who's never been a father. . . . Anyway
Along a father comes, discoursing as
He passes to a little he or she
That's borne, it happens, facing frontally.
The better to enjoy the view? One knows
Before it's made how one's objection goes:

That all that stands before the infant's eyes—
Span, spires beneath befleeced cerulean—
The infant no more sees for what it is
Than understands a word its father says.
Which doesn't stop the father's talk, or mean
That worlds aren't being taken in.

PETER CAMPION

Peter Campion was born in 1976 in Boston. He is the author of two books of poetry, *Other People* (University of Chicago Press, 2005) and *The Lions* (University of Chicago Press, 2009). He has also published a monograph on the painter Mitchell Johnson (Terrence Rogers Fine Art, 2004). His poems and prose have appeared in *ArtNews*, the *Boston Globe*, *Modern Painters*, the *New Republic*, *Poetry*, *Slate*, the *Yale Review*, and elsewhere. A former Stegner Fellow and Jones Lecturer at Stanford University, and a winner of the Pushcart Prize, he now teaches at Auburn University and edits the journal *Literary Imagination*. He lives in Auburn, Alabama.

Two Doubles

They wear our bodies unsuspectingly.
  Make love, or fight, and they don't know
that their lives go on like programs on TV
  we've muted.
                   But their gestures show
how she wheels around, trying not to trouble
  him with the sight of her smudged tears.

Or how his apologies fall to babble.
  Or how some clownish splutter tears
both of them up with laughter.
                    Are they meant
  to be our bodies in projection?

The life we live wholly as instrument
  beneath our souls' plot-mad direction?

No. Like slippery creatures they evade
  any one view of who they are.

Last night, our dwelling in the talk we made.
  Your story shushing us both far
into the wash of us. The living room
  that much more our warm retreat.

Then suddenly a dull, beam-rattling "boom!"
  Running outside to the puddled street
and craning
              from the house to the alleyway
  I caught the dent on the circuit box.
The wires shooting blue sparks in a circling spray.

Screeching
              toward neighboring blocks
the car that trailed smashed headlight glass behind.

Mist for a second flashed-through
                        clearer
and I saw (the memory's printed in my mind)
how they grinned together in the mirror.

"Or Whatever Your Destination May Be . . ."

Part glamorous, part penitential, tunnel
  follows tunnel. Then halls through the concourse.
  The fuselage. It's like long tubes that funnel
out through the dark, this exhilarated force
  so constant, even now, in the muffled light
  by my bed, to lull myself, I plot a course
of my own imagined networks through the night.

  Though they keep leading to that hellish hotel
  two weeks ago. Some couple's screaming fight.
  Then the low moans, more screaming.
                        Who could tell
  what room it came from? It came from the blaring stack
  of rooms. And listening to those voices swell
through the plaster, I thought I heard the halls in back
  of me give way:
              it seemed those people's souls
  themselves were swarming in a ragged pack
through a brambly, whacked-out maze of knolls
  and gullies.
            So tonight: of every place
I can call back, how weird that this one consoles

my amped brain the best.
                                When I turn to face
the glass, it's just our view of Berkshire Street.
The floodlit baseball park.
                                There's not a trace
of any nightmare forest.

        *

                        Except in this sweet
chill from the air conditioner, now I sense
what it is that assuaged me:
                                the more complete
calm, that came in a half dream, as my tense
body finally washed to sleep that night.

There was a meadow. And a chain-link fence
vanished to silver mesh above the height
we must have descended from. All around
those other faces quavered into sight.

Their shadows stretched across the littered ground.
Stretched as far as the glistering sign
of a city miles away.
                        The only sound
was the wind. Though pushing on
                                over the shine
off power stations and junkyards, you could see
those towers scale the long horizon line.

This Blue Vase

shows more than the morning clarities
of sun through leaves then through these windows.

Each thing is imbued by others. And staring
at the convex glass, I see the falls
in the one picture that held me enthralled
while you walked on through the gallery.

Even back then I must have felt
the photograph's stark black and white
trapping the glow off tons of water
in the entire minute of exposure
one hundred years before we were born
as weirdly relevant: how barns
and long gone houses' clapboard sides
above where shadowed cliff-face slid
vertiginously toward the falls
reflected all my naive bewilderment
seeing what I'd thought permanent
turn so starkly half unreal.

But this morning, watching sunlight steal
across this table's lacquered pine,
I still sense, through the smallest glints,
your presence still fusing all I see with you.
Blue irises from this vase's blue.

Vermont: The Ranch House

Uphill that day a coyote howled no end.
  And on neighbors' properties where they were penned
the hunting dogs went crazy. We could hear
  their barks, then echoes. Whether it was fear
or animal bliss, it sounded like mimicry.
  The dogs copied the cousin they couldn't see.
We paused to listen, ignored it. Words we'd flung

in anger minutes ago still hung
around the breezeway. Your relatives' house we stayed
  the weekend in, the remoteness, only made
the silence tenser: up against the house
  rage infected those blue and orange boughs.
It felt as if our feelings could be consoled
  only because they couldn't be controlled:
as if we couldn't speak till the landscape
  (gone for an instant strangely clear, each shape
outlined in blue, each leaf-edge wet and stark)
  finally lost all profile in the dark.

Or is that the way I want it in a poem?
  This urge to summon up your family home
must come from wanting to return to every scene
  where emotion floored me, so I can scrub them clean.

Later that evening, with the parlor lamp
  shut off, you allowed my fingers against your damp
cold cheek. And across the room each family photo,
  fluorescing through darkness, gave a glow
of animal warmth. Which seemed to break the chill.
  Seemed to flow from an instinct we didn't will.
And that silence no longer felt like a silence
  so much as our region of the hillside, dense
with sound. The dogs still scrabbled in their joy or fear.
  The open "hoo . . ." still echoed: thin and clear.

The Red Eye

After Hesiod

Even when the porthole was black I tried to scan
  for roads beside the page. And when they ran

to a slender row (like pixels linking to a string)
  I shut the book and stared below the wing.

So many times before, the same apportioned blaze
  must have rippled through space to hold my gaze.
Only this time, a newness infused the spreading grid.

  And the sense that this pulsing circuit hid
everyone I knew, that this mineral sluice was home,
  sank in when I turned back and read the poem.

My eyes dropped to the place where "snakes came out to mate.
  Scales dimly flashed.
                        Whether in love or hate
or both all tangled in their writhing ritual
  fangs slashed at hairless flesh, then drank their fill.

In the pits and in the tunnels, run-off dribbled down
  on speckled leaves.
                        And there beneath each town
and beneath even the clustered towers, molten souls
  swivelled and sliced through the mazes of snake-holes.

Eager to move inside whatever form they found,
  they rose toward being, up through the iced ground."

Poem before Sunrise

  This image of a hole
  planted behind my eyes.

  Swivelled whirlpool that curves
  right through me. Central bole

sawed from the tree of nerves.
This is the urge that lies

behind the throb of seeing.
This is the barest force

giving up to the wish
of whatever greater being:

little transparent fish
dragged on its one course

through forests of coral flowers
seeking the break of day.

Whatever way this power
pulls me: . . . ok . . . ok . . .

Magnolias

Ambition. Jealousy. Adrenaline.
The fear that loneliness is punishment
and that corrosive feeling draining down
the chest the natural and just result
of failures. . . . What delicious leisure not
to feel it. What sweet reprieve to linger
here with these ovals of purple and flamingo
plumed from the tree or splayed on pavement.
If only for these seconds before returning
to the open air those flowers keep
pushing out of themselves to die inside.

Big Avalanche Ravine

Just the warning light on a blue crane.
Just mountains. Just the mist that skimmed
them both and bled to silver rain
lashing the condominiums.
But there it sank on me. This urge
to carve a life from the long expanse.
To hold some ground against the surge
of sheer material. It was a tense
and persistent and metallic shiver.
And it stayed, that tremor, small and stark
as the noise of the hidden river
fluming its edge against the dark.

Recurring Dream in a New Home

Sumac and shadow of the girder bridges.
Then the downtown where a fountain's iron swan

gurgles white gouts. Beyond the buggy edges
fraying the green, the darkness switches on.

Solid as cups of buttermilk they stand
beside their Pontiac. Her polka dots

rumple and shine in the moonlight. His hand
pats a pocket for something he forgot.

I fumble toward them: "Nana! Boppa! It's me!
. . . We have our own son now!" They turn and stare

as if they sense someone they can't quite see.
And then they've given up. They're in their car.

Taillights smudge mist. And all they've left behind
is their image: the pudgy rectitude

of retirees venturing half blind
into their lives, not knowing what's ahead

except the increasing toil of taking on
bodies again, each morning, as the dark

slinks off behind the buildings and the sun
drips from the cars and trash and steaming bark.

BILL COYLE

Photo by Cattie Coyle

Bill Coyle was born in Bremerhaven, West Germany, in 1968. His book of poetry *The God of This World to His Prophet* (Ivan R. Dee) won the New Criterion Poetry Prize and was published in 2006. His translations from the Swedish have appeared in journals and anthologies such as *PN Review, Poetry, Poetry in Translation,* and *New European Poets* (Graywolf). He teaches English at Salem State College in Salem, Massachusetts. He lives in Somerville, Massachusetts.

Aubade

On a dead street
in a high wall
a wooden gate
I don't recall

ever seeing open
is today
and I who happen
to pass this way

in passing glimpse
a garden lit
by dark lamps
at the heart of it.

Kolmården Zoo

Over our heads, trailing a wake of air
and an enormous shadow as it passed,
the falcon glided to its trainer's fist
and settled like a loaded weapon there.

Then, while she fed the bird bit after bit
of . . . what? rabbit? the trainer gave her talk:
These birds, she said, prey on the small and weak,
adding for the children's benefit

that this, though it seems cruel, is really good
since otherwise the other rabbits, mice,
squirrels, what have you, would run out of space
and die of illness or a lack of food.

I know what she was trying to get across,
and I don't doubt it would be healthier
if we were more familiar than we are
with how the natural world draws life from loss;

and granted, nothing is more natural
than death incarnate falling from the sky;
and granted, it is better some should die,
however agonizingly, than all.

Still, to teach children this is how things go
is one thing, to insist that it is good
is something else—it is to make a god
of an unsatisfactory status quo,

this vicious circle that the clock hands draw
and quarter, while the serpent bites its tail,
or eats the dust, or strikes at someone's heel,
or winds up comprehended by a claw.

She launched the bird again. We watched it climb
out of the amphitheatre, headed toward
the darkened spires of a nearby wood,
then bank, then angle toward us one last time.

The God of This World to His Prophet

Go to the prosperous city,
for I have taken pity

on its inhabitants,
who drink and feast and dance

all night in lighted halls
yet know their bacchanals

lead nowhere in the end.
Go to them, now, commend,

to those with ears to hear,
a lifestyle more austere.

Tell all my children tired
of happiness desired

and never had that there
is solace in despair.

Say there is consolation
in ruins and ruination

beneath a harvest moon
that is itself a ruin,

comfort, however cold,
in grievances recalled

beside a fire dying
from lack of love and trying.

Living

In winter, once the ice on the lake is safe,
a group of local ice-fishers build a town
with houses, streets, a store, a tavern—
all the necessities—then move out there.

The Swallow Anthology of New American Poets

By day they wait for nothing they sense or see
until a line goes taut like a sudden thought,
   and someone lifts a flash of silver
      out of an opening in the surface.

With darkness, things are otherwise. Then the lights
that glitter on the shore they have left behind
   amount to a new constellation
      born in the lowliest part of heaven;

then sometime neighbors head to their tavern, where,
because they know the season is all too brief,
   they stay up later than they mean to,
      playing guitar, trading stories, drinking,

and feeling how expansive it strangely is
to have it all come down to this makeshift town
   then, closer, to this point, this tavern
      crowded with music and light and voices.

Past closing, now. The bartender, bound for what,
for the time being, is home, recollects the stars.
   Out of a pocket near his heart he
      fishes a flask of the local moonshine.

There is a dark below and a dark above;
The fish are darting stars, while the stars are schools
   that drift so glacially their slightest
      movement plays out over generations.

It is a private vision. Around him sleep
his customers and friends in their home-spun homes.
   He takes a measured swig of liquor,
      grimaces, grins. It is nearly daybreak.

Bill Coyle

Knowledge

Knowledge is found at the Know Ledge
high above all you know
and when you stand there scanning
the world below

it won't, for all its beauty,
be the phenomenal view
of foreign and familiar
that dazzles you—

mountains on the horizon
staggering toward the sun,
the flood-plains where your battles
were lost and won—

but how, when you stand on the Know Ledge,
and catch your breath and call
to the world you came from, crying
hello to it all,

you hear within the voices
echoing in reply
an emptiness allowing
for earth and sky.

The Soundman's Funeral

We honored his request, playing in lieu
of hymns or eulogies the sounds he made
    back in the old days, sounds that made
    the most unlikely tales ring true.

A squeal of brakes, a thunder-clap, a shot,
a locomotive's wail, coyotes crying.
    Some of the guests by then were crying,
    others, lost in the story, not.

Rain on a tin roof, a dog barking, boughs
groaning in a great wind. We thought of him,
    of all that found its voice through him.
    A door—the front door of a house?—

slammed and we listened as someone descended
a creaking stairway, opened a car door
    started the car up, shut the door,
    then drove off. So the story ended.

Or not the story, but that episode,
to be continued anytime we hear
    one of his trademark noises, hear
    a car pull past us on the road,

say, or a dog bark. Not that he's not gone,
but it may help, now that he's left this life,
    to hear him in the sounds of life,
    which is a show, and must go on.

Traveling Alone

Fetching a luggage wagon, I'm aware,
not for the first time on this journey, how
bizarre it is for me that you're not here,
that I can't turn and talk to you just now.

I know I shouldn't over-dramatize;
it's only going to mean a week away.

It isn't even, I now realize,
as If I'd anything that much to say,

aside from *I'll go grab a wagon*, which,
if you were here, you would assume I'd do.
And yet the fact that I can't mumble such
a consummate banality to you

and hear your equally mundane *all right*
makes me feel shut up inside my skin.
Nothing, not the others from the flight
shouldering for their baggage, nor the din

of intercom and small talk reaches me
(being neither here nor there) where I
am lost in thought, thinking how it will be
if you should be the first of us to die.

Summer's End

She's seated at a table on the back porch
picking stems from a bowl of cloudberries—
those gumball sized, hairy, nearly translucent
yellow berries one imagines Bosch,
as demiurge, being driven to invent
as prisons for his naked sensualists. She's

a little drunk, again, but it's past noon,
she's on vacation, and trust her, you don't want to
lecture her on this; you don't understand,
no one does, how his betrayal—No one.
A yellow-jacket hangs from her left hand.
She smiles, whispers to it, *You love me, don't you?*

A Mouse

It crouches, what is left of it, in a corner of the terrace,
the length of my index finger and just
taller than my hand with the palm face down.

Its bones are white and rough but delicate,
like limestone or seashell, or coral or snow.
It must have crouched all winter here.

Still as stone, it resembles nothing
so much as one of those balsawood skeletons—
of dinosaurs, typically—that children assemble.

Fearing death would hear it, it held its breath,
then stilled its heartbeat; fearing death would scent it,
it distributed its flesh to the ants for safe keeping.

It made a little bed of dust
and leaves and the brittle hulls of insects;
it lay awake, sensing death near.

When death stopped by, he stooped to consider it,
and taking it for one of his harmless creatures,
left a few seed husks to tide it over.

Hindsight

But is it really necessary I
renounce all of his works? Couldn't I just
renounce the vast majority of them?
We were out walking, you were explaining why
you couldn't quite convert. I was nonplussed.

Theologically, I could condemn
what seemed to me a clear misunderstanding
of the relationship of good and evil,
but in esthetic terms I understood:
Given that you imagined God commanding
all that was light and airy and the devil
all that was dark and dangerous, pure good
had to be lethal, both in life and art.
I think I still believe that, in my heart.

MORRI CREECH

Morri Creech was born in Moncks Corner, South Carolina, in 1970, and was educated at Winthrop University and McNeese State University. He currently lives in Charlotte, North Carolina, where he teaches creative writing at Queens University of Charlotte. He has published two collections of poetry, *Paper Cathedrals* (Kent State University Press, 2001), which won the 2000 Stan and Tom Wick Poetry Prize, and *Field Knowledge* (Waywiser, 2006), which won the first annual Anthony Hecht Poetry Prize in 2005. He has also written two books in collaboration with the photographers Robert ParkeHarrison and Shana ParkeHarrison, *Listening to the Earth* and *The Book of Life* (21st). He has received a 2007 National Endowment for the Arts Fellowship, a Ruth Lilly Fellowship from *Poetry Magazine* and the Modern Poetry Foundation, and an artist's fellowship from the Louisiana Division of the Arts.

Engine Work: Variations

June morning. Sunlight flashes through the pines.
Blue jays razz and bicker, perch on a fence post
back of my grandfather's yard. His stripped engines
clutter the lawn. And everywhere the taste
of scuppernongs just moments off the vines,
so sour that you would swear the mind has traced
a pathway through the thicket, swear the past
comes clear again, picked piecemeal from the dust—.

~

Or else it's late—September—and the shade
thicker than I recall: those cardinals,
finches or mockingbirds still haven't made
a sound all afternoon, though ripe fruit swells
on bough, or branch—or bramble. Thus the frayed
edge of recollection slowly ravels
away to nothing, until that place is gone
where the heart would know its object, and be known.

~

All right. Not to begin with those backlit pines,
those scuppernongs, the jay perched on a branch
of sweet gum—no, oak, I think. With what, then?
With my grandfather holding a torque wrench
or ratchet? Some old engine's stammer and whine
before it starts, or doesn't—a house finch,
singing or silent? Language, too, seems wrong,
though it's all I have. *Grandfather. Scuppernong.*

~

To fix him in some moment, word for word,
that man who taught me gears and cylinders, sweat,

precision of machinery—the hard
love of assembling things.
                    I know the heat
all summer hung like a scrim where pistons fired
and the boy I was watched in the raw sunlight.
Spilled oil rainbowed in its shallow pan.
One bird call, maybe; fruit on a trellised vine . . .

                        ~

Impossible not to change things, move the words
from here to there. It's late now. Nothing's settled—
not engine noise or the sound of one far bird
the mind sings true. Which version of the world
should I believe? This morning in the yard
scuppernongs hang and sweeten. Pine boughs yield
some fragment of the blue jay's call, a sound
the resonant air repeats but cannot mend.

Banking Hours

Time to get down to business. Time to settle
            Accounts and round the sums.
    The sun's loose change lies scattered on the floor
And shade has inched between the pansies and the mums.
    The piper's all played out, the whore's been diddled,
            And the shops have closed their doors.

                    ———

Time to square with the clock's big jaundiced eye
            As it glares back at you;
    With those two sweeping hands that meet like shears
When you wake up not sure yet if the dream was true.
    Time to answer the phone and tell us why
            Your payments are in arrears.

                    ———

Time to admit the check was never "in
                    The mail," that you were never
          "Between jobs currently," nor was your card
Mischarged, stolen, lost. You've always been too clever.
          You've always had a tendency to spend
                    More than you could afford.

———

          How easily you fall for cheap distractions:
                    Long nights, gossip and girls,
          The highball tumbler sweating along its facets.
How easily, old swine, you fritter away your pearls
          For one more chance to nose the world's confections,
                    Squandering your assets,

———

          Until look, it's late: the leaves have gone the way
                    Of dames and dollars now.
          The spider's tallied up her last gauze beads
On the web strung between the porch and locust bough.
          That wind sounds like the rake of a croupier
                    Combing the yellow weeds.

———

          So run the spreadsheets. Balance the register.
                    You knew, of course—didn't you?—
          The bill would post, that notice for both prime
And principal: Records Show. Please Pay Amount Due.
          It's time to make good with your creditor.
                    Soon ends will meet. It's time,

          Dear customer, it's time.

Gleanings

For Hattie

To see them for what they are, not to make
more of them than the afternoon allows:
starlings among the sweet gum limbs, a rake
propped beneath those leaves the wind will take,
my child gathering feathers beside the house—
a sleight of season, when some moment scatters
its riches across the lawn. Nothing to do
with dates or futures and, I'd guess, small matter
in the year's turning.

                But I remember, too,
a thousand starlings in my father's yard,
his Chevy in the drive, a smell of leaves
clear as the feather in my daughter's hand—
a swatch of consequence the mind weaves
from history and chance, so that it's hard,
watching it all, not to construe some meaning
from starling, rake, limb, leaf, the child who stands
gathering feathers beneath the shade of wings.

The Canto of Ulysses

Primo Levi, in his apartment in Turin,
reading *The Divine Comedy*. February, 1987

Drowsing, head propped above the eighth circle,
he feels the present shifting like a keel,
takes his bearings by the toss and swivel

of snow in window light—though still less real,
it seems to him, than that thick Polish snow
which, tumbling in his mind, begins to wheel

like Dante's leaves or starlings, like the slow
stumble of shades from an open freight car,
or from an open book. All night, the snow

whirls at his window, whiting out the stars.
We sailed now for the stars of that other pole.
Leafing a thumb-worn page, he tries to parse

those lines he once struggled to recall
for a fellow prisoner, who'd hoped to learn
Italian as they scraped rust from the wall

of an emptied petrol tank. *The greater horn
began to mutter and move, as a wavering flame
wrestles against the wind and is overworn—*

although, oddly enough, the lines sound tame
now there is no one to explain them to.
Nor words to write. His own canticle of pain

is, after all, finished. The past is nothing new.
And the present breaks over him like the dream
of firelight, plush eiderdown, and hot stew

a prisoner will sometimes startle from
who has lost hope of returning to the world,
blowing upon his hands the pluming steam

of breath, in which a few snowflakes are whirled.
Or, nodding above the passage where Ulysses
tells how the second journey ended—hurled

by a *fierce squall,* till *the sea closed over us—*
he feels at the moment like that restless king
home from Troy after twenty years, his face

grown old and strange from so much wandering,
who broods all night over the cyclops' lair
or Circe's pigs, the shades' dim gathering,

then falls asleep.
                    He leans back in his chair.
It all seems now just like it seemed—the snow;
the frozen dead. They whisper on the stair

as if he'd called their shades up from below
to hear the story of Agamemnon slain,
or paced out the long maze of the *Inferno*

to hear their lamentations fresh again.
Beyond his window: stars, the sleeping town,
the past, whirled like flakes on a windowpane—

the sea closed over us, and the prow went down.
Dreaming, he drops the book without a sound.

The Trouble

It seems these days you've had enough of order.
For months you harried the blackbirds from the yard
with a pellet gun, clatter of pie tins, an absurd
straw-stuffed overcoat, and gave no quarter,
chucking lit fireworks, once, to chase them off
the laundry poles and apple trees. And now?
The pump gun leans against the table saw
in your garage, the clean shirts billow and luff
in mild suburban peace, although the change
has quite unsettled you. It's true the lawn
looks clear, the trees untroubled. But at dawn

sometimes you hear the creaking of a hinge,
a swing set or a screen door, and you wake
thinking they might be there. Of course, they're not.
They linger at the margins of your thought
like a dream you had once but can't seem to shake,
and now you wake so often, that each time
wind sifts the limbs or flaps the empty sleeves
you want to tear them down, scatter the leaves
you spent all season raking into prim
heaps near the road, then stand out in the cold
beneath clouds of a slowly changing weather
and watch the pale sky darken to a feather,
until the meaning wings down and takes hold.

World Enough

Swift as a weaver's shuttle, time unspools
           its hours in glistening threads
and rapturous polychromes—in the arc of leaf
           or feather toward the pools
of that deep shade to which the morning weds
           its brilliance, in a brief

slur of redwings above the white-washed fence,
           the sprinkler's lisp and hiss
trailing a veil of diamond through the air—
           and spins a present tense
of such dizzying concords one is apt to miss
           much of the affair.

Think of those vast histories that have gone
           unnoticed or unseen:

ants marching on some martial expedition,
        defending their Babylon
of mounds and chambered catacombs between
        the posts of the Crucifixion,

bees building their honey in the walls
        at Jericho or Troy—
whole catalogs of kingdoms and empires,
        straw-built citadels,
Spenglerian cycles of health and slow decay,
        all lost in the spangled fires

of daylight, the rich flux of hours and years.
        Amid such dense detail
it's easy to miss the moment when Atropos
        bends close with her shears
to cut the taut threads, until their tensions fail
        and time's grip turns loose;

easy, in Eden's commerce of sunlight,
        wild fruit and stippled wings,
to miss the cormorant bristling on the bough.
        So once a man lost sight,
near Pompeii, of history's beginnings,
        caught in some lavish *now*

of appetite—the flush of sex, the steam
        rising from his bathwater—
in all that languor failing to note the wind
        stir the trickled streams
along his flanks, the mountain sound its thunder,
        or those first warm snows descend.

Erica Dawson was born in Columbia, Maryland, in 1979. Her book of poems, *Big-Eyed Afraid* (Waywiser, 2007), won the 2006 Anthony Hecht Poetry Prize. Her poems have appeared or are forthcoming in *Southwest Review, Harvard Review*, and *The Best American Poetry 2008*, among other journals and anthologies. She lives in Ohio, where she is pursuing a PhD in English from the University of Cincinnati.

God Girl

I was born (*again?!*) two times:
Christened, then second dipped in a luke-
Warm pool with *Satan, I rebuke*
Thee, saved with pantomimes

(Hand down, across) and breath
Held with the Holy Ghost before
The family and the flock. Once more,
Bear me again. In death,

I'm good. At church, the hat
Appeared as a centerpiece of lace-
Wrapped buds. I watched the angel face
Stained in the ziggurat-

Like tiers of storied glass
Go flush in the sun, turn corpse-opaque
With clouds. And I, for heaven's sake,
Took heaven's biomass,

Washing feet first in the church-
White basement, hosed and pedicured.
I held the shot-glassed blood and stirred
Beside the Eden birch

Weeping to baked-in grass,
Green as a crayon. My fingertip
Went plum. Mom: *God, girl, take a sip*
Already. The church, en masse:

Amen. Good Lord. God Girl.
I love that end to the final verse,

Revelation to Genesis, Eve's curse
In blood, the sidewalk twirl

Of sisters in Gunne Sax
Chiffon, Ham's myth, and that dark dream
Where lepers lose their limbs, each ream
Of Bible type in black,

The Jesus red, the cracks
In the varnished pew, but most, the knell—
Less bleak than Longfellow's wailing bell
And forlorn amphibrachs,

But chimes the same for death,
I Do, or simply Sunday mass.
That bell, reverberating glass,
Is like an isopleth

Connecting day to day,
Ringing it New. And when the hearse
Carries me home, recite this verse,
This is my body, and say

I'm sacrilege in my
Best dress, God bless, and off to Hell
For that I shalt not ever tell.
Remember me as I

Go under, over, pass
And turn to Old, from God's Sweet Pea
Thrice born, in bone twice souled, to three
In liquid, solid, gas.

High Heel

I was born, Mom says, bull's eye
Parfait, without a flaw—reflex
And one repro of fine she-sex—
All lash and rock-a-bye-

Full lids looking to close.
Slim collarbone, and rosebud pout,
I'm Queen without a Doubt
Of all hatched embryos.

Long may I reign with a spine
Perfected in its curvature's
Half curlicue and constant manicures
On two flat feet. I line

My ankles up and, see,
They propinquate. They roll until
They collapse. The missing insteps spill
From the slingbacks' nudity

And barest ties. So call
Me Mary Jane with a turf toe fetish.
I'm stacked. With three-inch-high coquettish
Stilettos, I'm Belle o' the Ball

And socket joint. *There goes
High Heel.* I've heard my ankles crack
And traced the point where I go black
To white on all ten toes

(Top brown to bottom peach)
As if my foot's biracial. In

The lady's pump, I'm genuine
Sunday Best (Praise Jesus! Preach!).

I'm the club's platforms. And though
I'll never arabesque *en pointe*,
I stand, bipodal, to disappoint
With all this bod, dance the foe

's faux *pas de deux* with the full-
Length mirror. I'm patent, polished, buffed,
Strap-bound, and muled. I'm powderpuffed.
I'm pinched. With a push and pull,

I make my blisters pop
In a serous ooze. If I could name
The foot's small bones, I'd play a game
And count the talus, cop

The dice and cuneiform,
The mid-foot characters (the wedges
Somewhere beneath the thong's thin edges),
The cuboid, and linguiform

Long toes in dual tones.
My skeleton is narratory,
Completely born and half a story
Writ large in genes and bones.

Credo

As a woman, I have learned
Some men are really bad

At whispering, as if
Their tenors can't be tempered,

Slight winds, perhaps, more apt
At fine seduction. Still,

Give me their manly lows,
The broader pitch of *Os*,

Pharynx tremors, and hard
Gs. Now I've come to think

Their throats are coated red,
Bright red, engorged, a sinew

Of veins across their necks
When they inflect a sound

And swallow, understood.
Though something should be said

For breath, an *h* unseen
In *God*, lipped in *Come here*,

My mouth is big. I think
I'm ready for my manhood.

Exam Room Three

> If I could be nineteen again . . .
> At twenty-two you're dead.

I heard that notion in my head,
Sitting in the orange chair and flipping through
A *Woman's Day* from 1996. A stocky nurse
Appeared. She led me to

Exam Room Three and showed me where to lay my purse.
The room was warm. My face was red.
I got undressed.

Biting my lower lip, I tried
To hold back tears. The needle poked, slid in
My breast. The paper gown tucked underneath my arm
      made a crink-
ling noise. I flinched. My skin
Burned as he eased it out, then in again. "I think
The odds are clearly on our side,"
The doctor stressed.

A week was packed in every day,
Or so it seemed, waiting. I can't think back
To how it felt. I think of how it was, the way the light
Bulb died, the useless stack
Of magazines I bought to fill the time, the night
He called, the word "benign." I play
A game and test

Myself, again. I picture me,
A gurney in a sterile room the day
I finally die: the masks, the I-V drugs, cold, slow inside
My veins, the chills, the way
The disinfectant lingers there. And fear? I hide
From that. I give myself a C.
Average. At best.

Busy Man

If Busy Man wears many hats
Then someone get me one big ol'

Sombrero—just one job, the cat's
Big dog meow to one who stole
The gist but never skimmed the whole
Dang self-help book in Border's half-
Off section,

          novice, like a calf
Stumbling to its knees when I go down
Like a heifer, hoarding crap to put
Beneath my tongue: threads from brown
Carpet or the wide-ruled notepad's foot
Of poetry—all work—and soot—
And play—picked off a match after I bate
My breath and blow and so regurgitate
My breath as smoke.

            The more I eat
The more I grab, and gorge, until
On Monday Dr. Misconceit
Plates up a dose of Seroquel—
Just one. You take JUST ONE.—for ill-
Fated but *No . . . no . . . NOT . . . psychotic. . . .*
(Sweet Boy and I prefer *exotic.*)
He says, *My god, you're done for. Sleep.*

I listen, but, in threes, I hear
The Nutcracker's last bars, the creep
To the end as Gelsey Kirkland's sheer
Nightgown slowly sways and the queer
Phrasing spins eddies spun not fast
Enough. (For parallax . . . at last
It's done.) *Say what, i.e., what God?*
I ask.

        Well, He don't sleep. He's at
His padlocked gates, laid back with an odd

Expression and his trilby hat
Cocked low. He winks, and I know that,
That, God, that God . . . THAT God still waits
For Sunday's off and recreates
Since God must go a little crazy,
Too, when the night skies in between
Columbus and here don't appear as hazy
Or dark, but bleed like a knifed-up scene,
Like bludgeon rust and swaddling, clean
White gauze.
                    He's up and at it again.
He needs a piss, another pen
For names, more names, just one last name
In His book. His wrinkled hand is cramped
To a claw or shaped in a hellish flame,
Or teardrop, yes, the one that damps
The spark when, back at work, my lamp's
Burned out and I strike strike strike the thin
Long match and scorch my chin
To taste the smell of my own skin—

Press on, Busy Man. Press on. Chew through
Your cheek and do it right, your grin
Like hunted hides, drenched in its true
Colors. Grind down to the bone; gnash; spew
Supper, search high and low for your halo and penance
And a murder of crows and your birthday's sentence.

BEN DOWNING

Photo by Jennifer Downing

Ben Downing was born in North Adams, Massachusetts, in 1967. His one book of poetry so far is *The Calligraphy Shop* (Zoo, 2003). He is coeditor of *Parnassus: Poetry in Review;* has taught at Columbia, Bryn Mawr, and the 92nd Street Y; and writes frequently for the *New Criterion*, the *Wall Street Journal*, and other publications. He lives in New York City.

Inshallah

—which is to say "God willing," more or less:
a phrase that rose routinely to her lips
whenever plans were hatched or hopes expressed,
the way we knock on wood, yet fervently,
as if to wax too confident might be
to kill the very thing she wanted most.
It used to pique and trouble me somehow,
this precautionary tic of hers, but now
I understand why she was skeptical
of what Allah in His caprice allots,
because that she should live He did not will,
or, more terribly, He did that she should not.

i.m. Mirel Sayinsoy 1967–99

Domestic Cappadocia

I

They seemed content enough, the married pair
who owned my charming cave hotel,
and ran the place commendably well,
solicitous yet casual, always there

when needed yet never hovering,
and often snatching (where they could)
quick private moments when they would
allow themselves some little couple thing

—a squeeze of hands, a whispered joke
or endearment, once even a furtive kiss—

that made their life appear harmonious.
Until, that is, the night I awoke

at three o'clock to yells and cries
rumbling up from their rooms below;
sporadic at first and fairly low-
intensity, they became by five

continuous, hysterical, and loud,
culminating in a door flung wide,
the wife's wails further amplified,
the husband's now-threatening shouts,

her frantic steps across the floor,
his execrations, her disdain,
a slap, a crash, a howl of pain,
the throwing open of another door

and then its slamming shut, as she,
escaping the hotel, at last broke free.

II

Eruptions were the making of this place:
thirty million years ago,
volcanoes smothered its plateau
in ash that hardened to a carapace

of tuff, which then, over untold time,
the wind and water whittled and tweaked
into a landscape so unique,
grotesque, and bizarrely sublime

as to look conjured up by mescaline,
with fairy chimneys, as they're known

—eroded pillars of multihued stone—
sprouting in their freakish thousands;

priapic yet mushroomy,
disposed in mazelike forests, they seem
a half-baked collaboration between
God, Freud, and Antonio Gaudí.

And its singularity does not end there:
the softness of the rock allowed
inhabitants to scoop and gouge
out spacious dwellings in midair,

and spurred the early Christians to go on
a binge of righteous burrowing, to honeycomb
the stacks with churches—frescoed, domed—
and monasteries by the dozen,

their materials purely Miocene,
their style Cro-Magnon-cum-Byzantine.

III

Exploring Cappadocia the next day,
the row still ringing harshly in my ears,
I couldn't help but find its atmosphere
impinged on by the ricochets

of last night's matrimonial misery,
which seemed to carom off the valley walls
and echo down the barrel vaults,
until the whole place became for me

a massive metaphor for marriage,
its formations analogous,
in their towering ungainliness,
to the virtual topography that rage

and love and other shaping elements
carve out wherever man and wife
attempt to fuse within a common life
their separate energies, and to cement,

from each one's detritus and lapilli
and fractured ancient bedrock and far-flung tuff,
some joint conglomerate strong enough
to serve as matter for the paradise

they plan to make of their terrain,
the formal garden almost Japanese
in its arrangement of their congeries—
exquisite, tranquil, eminently sane;

instead they wind up with a wilderness
of anfractuous ravines and random spikes.
Or so I grimly reckoned as I hiked,
my hoteliers' unholy mess

distending out to circumscribe
all foredoomed Adams and all Eves,
their union fundamentally misconceived.
Pausing, I looked afresh at the hive-

like monastic warrens in the rock above,
the chimney chapels and hermits' retreats,

and found myself in envy of such neat
withdrawal from the snares of worldly love.

What did they know, these celibates,
of feminine reproaches and bitter bedroom fights?
A happier breed of troglodytes
they must have been than we who set

our hopes on conjugal felicity,
we carnal cavemen who, in our primitive
compulsion foolishly to try and live
at peace with womankind, can never be

quite sure of the ground beneath our socks,
incessantly shifting as it is.
Within those Eris-haunted labyrinths
of stone and feeling interlocked

I wandered brooding for a time,
but then abruptly something gave,
and from then on I saw a different way.
The August sun, in its decline,

was coaxing warm new subtleties of tint
from a sea of twisting turrets, and so
majestic were they all aglow,
basking in their warped magnificence,

that they seemed to stand in roseate
contradiction of my metaphor,
or rather to deplore
the bleak terms in which I figured it.

"If we are like marriage," they collectively said,
"it is not in that our tortured piles of ash

evoke your human proneness always to rehash
old grievances; if we are to be read,

O tiny pessimist, as a parable
of what happens when husbands and wives
combine the landscapes of their lives,
it must be because we are supremely beautiful,

an involute and cloistered little universe
of time-cut spires and chasms—as is marriage."
Thus rebuked, I came to like what I'd disparaged,
to view as more a windfall than a curse

the fact that we instinctively cooperate
in fashioning our own mad tortuous
geology, invisible to all but us,
a thing of weird yet captivating shapes.

Solvitur ambulando. I noticed now
what had eluded me before: the vines
that yield the region's tolerably good wines,
growing here and there, and the heavy-boughed

occasional small orchard, dense with fruit;
for the rich volcanic soil was driving up,
in the few farmable spots, a bumper crop,
planted not by monks hell-bent on beatitude

but by ordinary Turks from nearby towns,
domestic, familial, making their homes
in hollowed-out stalagmites whose mild stone
is forever being weathered splendidly down.

Calle Plácida Luz de la Luna

"Street of Placid Moonlight"? Gimme a break.
My aunt's Arizona subdivision
summoned all my Manhattan derision
—how corny, how gringo, how fake!

But when one night I took my daughter
out for a walk, the moon rode high, and lo,
the even sheen it cast across the faux-
adobe houses, and the way it caught her

exuberant small face, upturned in wonderment,
filled me with the kind of mild serenity
that had, coyote-like, eluded me
in every tranquil desert place we went;

not among the ironwoods and saguaros
but within that synthetic so-called estate
I found calm indifference to the laws of fate
and a sudden lifting of all sorrows.

Past stagy aloes and transplanted mesquites,
beneath a cliché-encrusted moon,
we pottered along, perfectly in tune—
with what happy steps we walked those placid streets.

Public Transit

Aboard the train, the usual thing:
a conversation overheard,
then eavesdropped on: two friends
discussing an absent third,

their heads ashake with sympathy,
in shared concern their voices hushed;
so that I caught, for all my strain,
no more than snatches as we rushed

downtown. At first one word, "... divorce ...,"
its steely second syllable
landing like a guillotine,
alone cut through the shrill

disharmony of track and wheel;
but then during a smoother stretch
whole phrases reached my ear:
it seems he'd chanced upon—poor wretch!—

"... his wife in bed with someone else ..."
and that "... his daughter has Tourette's...."
And there I was, attending to
the woes of a man I'd never met,

whose very name I failed to learn;
yet all the while half-thinking of
my eight-months-pregnant wife, and how
the vulnerabilities of love

would soon, for me, be doubled;
and wondering whether I,
when sorrows come (as Claudius says)
no longer single spies

but in ruinous battalions,
can possibly withstand their force;
and whether anyone, in fact,
dare doubt that in due course

Ben Downing

they'll be the sad case talked about,
their life careering off the rails:
the one regarding whom such friends
as these, in view of his travails,

will some day ask quite hopelessly
—this last bit gleaned before we all
stand up, get off, disperse—
" . . . Who can catch him if he falls? . . ."

Two Husbands

i)

The opposite of Prospero,
Rossetti disinterred his book.
Those sonnets he'd consigned below,
trussed up so fondly with a lock
of his wife's lamented golden hair,
now seemed to him a pentateuch,
a very grimoire rashly buried.
With ghoulish verve he undertook
his mouldered volume to retrieve,
then published it to much acclaim.
One moral is you shouldn't leave
the things of love with those of fame,
confusing them in coffinwood;
another's that you damn well should.

ii)

To bolt in shock, as Ruskin did,
on meeting with a hirsute mons

might seem a radical response.
But when you think that caryatids,

demure madonnas, glabrous nymphs
were all he'd known of womankind,
it's no surprise that he should find
his own endowment going limp,

eclipsing thus his honeymoon.
Poor John, he's taken heat enough
for having failed before the muff.
Yet who among us dare impugn

his quaint ideal of furlessness?
Who can endure, with firm sangfroid,
the finding of some beastly flaw
in one's anticipated bliss?

His case enjoins us to forswear
the perfect flesh unfollicled
and to accept, once and for all,
that everything in life has hair.

Ben Downing

ANDREW FELD

Photo by Nick Twemlow

Andrew Feld was born in 1961 in Cambridge, Massachusetts. He is the author of *Citizen* (HarperCollins, 2004), a 2003 National Poetry Series selection, chosen by Ellen Bryant Voigt. He holds an MFA from the University of Houston and has received a Wallace Stegner Fellowship from Stanford University. His other honors include a James Michener Foundation grant, the Discovery/The Nation award, two Pushcart Prizes, and inclusion in the Best American Poetry series. His poetry has appeared in the *Canary*, *Poetry*, *Tikkun*, *TriQuarterly*, and many other journals. He is an assistant professor at the University of Washington and the editor in chief of the *Seattle Review*. He lives in Seattle with his wife, Pimone Triplett, and their son, Lukas.

On Fire

Having been taught by fools, how else could I have ended up
but as I am? a man who panics at the sound of his own voice,
a blusterer, afraid that within the five-pointed maple leaf there lies
another name he never knew; ready, always, to be found wrong.

Listen: in my tenth year they put me in a room where one plane
watched another plane fly over a city. It was morning in both
places. In black & white at first the explosion looked like water
rising. Captured, they say, on film, as in: pulled out of time

so we can rewind it and watch it happen again, as in a memory,
as in: this is a memory we all have, these are our family pictures.
There was that kind of shame. As if the fire really had been stolen.
And sitting on the floor there was one boy who even earlier

that year came home to find his mother hanging from a rope
in the kitchen. What didn't he know that he needed this film
to teach him? Already what he knew was enough to terrify
the teachers, so that they couldn't look at him. But they also

couldn't not look at him. As if he was an obscene pleasure.
And he was beautiful. Complete. But what he carried in him
seeped out as hate for anyone of the same sex as his mother.
It was that simple: even a fourth-grade mind could understand.

So the girls stayed away. And from the other side of the common
room, where the books full of numbers being added, subtracted
and divided were kept, our new teacher watched, helpless, knowing
he also needed this knowledge, but she couldn't give it to him.

Which might be why she let me touch her. Because she couldn't
get near him and my head against the antique white lace of her

dress was a good enough *almost*. Her hair was light brown, if I
remember correctly. *Innocent* is supposed to mean *free from hurt*

but it can also mean you don't know what you're doing. As when
I felt that touching her wasn't enough and I wanted to press closer,
until someone felt pain, or until I passed through her dress and found
myself inside her. It didn't matter if she was an adult and I was ten:

what I wanted wasn't sex. Or not what I have learned to think *sex*
is. Her dress was made of a material called *vintage*, which meant
that although it had managed to avoid all the minor catastrophes
of red wine stain and hook snag, along with the major disasters

of history, no one had treated the cloth with chemicals, to make it
flame retardant. And on the whole length of the hand-sewn inner seam
that started at her wrist and ran all the way down to her ankle,
no one had remembered to place even one small label warning:

if you touch the sleeve of this garment to the still-hot coils
of an electric stove, it will explode. Which is what happened.
There's the kind of scream you hear in movies. What I heard
twenty-seven years ago didn't sound anything like that. It was

sharper and can't be recorded. No matter how many times
you rewind the film. You keep going back and each time
there's a little less there. Until the memory has become
the event. And how you feel about the memory. The materials

have burnt away. There was so much fabric and all of it on fire.
Her hair too, which was long, as I remember. She came running
from the faculty kitchen, as if she could escape what she was
turning into. But all she did was excite and encourage the flames.

Ice Age

The sharp face of Mt. Olympus rises
above the glacial cape wrapped around
its neck: a climber's paradise, which I'm not
skilled enough to ascend. So I hike on
a ridge on the other side of the valley,
at a lesser though still great height, balanced
between the green and white—the rain forest
below me on my left, and on my right
a glacier, blinding in the August sun.
I stop to drink and, because I'm living
a clumsy life, drop my water-bottle cap
into the *bergshrund*—the gap where the ice
has pulled away from the mountain wall.
What happens next? Do I go in thirst among
the rocks, or walk carefully holding my water
upright? No. Instead, I lower myself
down into the real abyss. This happened.
I down-climbed through the day. The light turned blue,
then milky white, then a dark gray. The rock
in my hands was slick from the melting glacier.
I slipped, and fell, and clung, then slipped again
and stuck. Thirty or forty feet below the surface,
the snow was black with dirt and hard. Years,
millenniums, of weather were piled above me.
Who comes back from these places? Alive, down
there I thought *old world, new world*, and so,
this is where the time goes. But, mostly:
*what, exactly, is the stupidest thing
I've ever done?* Just what was beneath me?
A frozen field, with small, unnamed flowers,
caught in the summer when the snow fell

and didn't melt. Ever. As though at the ocean
a wave came in and stayed. And then another.
And so. The water walking up its own steps.
Is it better to freeze or drown? I up-climbed;
but even in the heat and green life of the rain
forest, where mosses hang on all the trees,
I still felt cold. In my mind, snow was falling
and sticking. It starts. Again. It's starting now.

The Boxers

Here, in the middle of all this Houston heat, the two
sixteen-year-old feather-weights step-by-stepping around
a center which should be large enough to hold them both

are working out, with painful, close attention, a number
of terrible ideas. The heat in here is an idea: it has a purpose
and a taste: it tastes like mile after mile of train passing

by the chicken-wired windows, the endless linked cars
full of what you don't know. The idea is that suffering
teaches you to suffer well, as though the end result

of dehydration isn't the skin & kidneys closing up
until what the body holds turns toxic, but the appearance
of something new willed into the blood, made of pain,

which you can then direct at the only person in the building
as beautiful as you are. Although of course there's nothing
sexual about this, the brief embrace of two boys, wet

with the same water you'd find at the bottom of any ocean.
And from the benches their plain-faced girlfriends watch, deep
in their impenetrable adolescence. As if all this was on t.v.,

as normal as the newsman saying *a train carrying industrial*
waste has derailed and is burning outside the city, and the simple
precautions: *Stay indoors. Close your windows. Don't breathe.*

But those two boys are in it, the sweat washing down
their stomachs and backs rinsing the black air off their skin,
turning the absurd abstractions of last night's news

into visible concentric rings around the waistbands
of their nylon Everlast shorts, as if all this was designed
to be a further test of their endurance, or show us

how even while you sleep your body can be making
serious mistakes, taking in lungful after lungful
of other people's errors. The soaked fabric sticks

to their thighs so closely you can see the hairs
underneath and the moving weave of muscle and almost
the tight string stitched through the over-lapping plates

of stomach muscle and cinched tight between them,
drawing them closer until the old men outside the ring
begin to shout they didn't come here to see lovers

and another man comes in to pull them apart.

Late Breather

> But words came halting forth . . .

He came from there not red and howling his one note
like all the rest. And so we had to worry. For years
he didn't cry. Or speak. Until, with such strange fears

and panic-quickened hearts, our senses finally woke
to what he meant. So long unheard he'd spoken in
the thirty-seven different dialects of rain
and all the languages of frost, shrinking in sun
or growing scratch by scratch upon the windowpane.

We'll wait. And when he finds the fragile hiss of mist
no longer answers to his growing needs, we'll tell
him what to say, instead of the thing itself. We'll twist
his tongue around our consonants and syllables.
We'll force our language down his throat, until he spits
it back at us. He'll have to take our words for it.

Crying Uncle

The sun is empty. Behind that great husk of light,
those brilliant surface-effects, a brutal, cold wind
of memory—Siberian, Tartar, *Poilische*—cuts through
the thin sweaters old Jewish men wear in Arizona,

cashmere, in bright shades of sherbet: orange, raspberry,
lemon and lime. And thinner, softer than the sunset-cloud
colored fleeces which adorn them, are their names,
which are retired now and wait, impatiently, for nothing.

My father's name is Maury. He had three brothers:
Meyer, Bernie and Marvin, all now deceased. As dead
weights on the page my desk lamp cranes its neck
to light upon, they file into the dark of an empty theater,

where the hand-wringing and grandiloquent gestures,
the gaslights and greasepaint, *Shylock's Daughter*

and powdered hair, where even the language has become
an embarrassment. And I'm working late with nothing

but these names to go by. Because I'm sitting Shivah here,
and my lamp is a soul, *animula*, little wanderer, and this is
the House of Mourning. For Meyer in Los Angeles,
a traffic engineer who changed his name to Myron X. and left

his television on day and night, for Marvin in Phoenix,
a landscape architect, and for Bernie, the man who set
the Doomsday Clock, a physicist: Manhattan Project,
Los Alamos, then MIT and *The Bulletin of Atomic Scientists*.

Their bodies and ashes are strewn across the continent:
Los Angeles, Phoenix, New York. In death they have been
utterly assimilated. And if they re-entered this world,
stripped clean of their Poland of Memories, of Isaac Babel's

"dense melancholy of Sabbath eves," their old men's bodies,
soft, sloping shoulders, their cancers and bad hearts,
what then? Would they come back holding little mirrors
and puff-pads, almost-angels in white laboratory coats,

scented of *Eternity* and offering, for next to nothing really,
to erase the years from around your eyes, flashing
your own face at you as if it was a postcard from Hell,
or would their transmigration take a wayward course,

treading again the ancestral paths of exile, through suburbs
of K- and Wal-Marts, limbo-landscapes the imagination
cannot stick to, until angry and complaining
they emerge from the long tunnel of birth. Am I them?

Meyer, Bernie, Marvin: one, two, three steps of a man
coming up from underground, sliding each shoe

over the worn steel lips of the subway stairs and holding
tightly to the handrail until, reassured by sound and feel,

once again he's walking the streets of his childhood.
They haven't cleaned the store windows but inside
leather and paper have turned to plastic and the language
that replaced his has been replaced by yet another.

No one remembers him now except the Cossack
lying on his newspaper bier, the one on the vodka bottle,
and the scholar of mislaid origins, bent all night over
a book with letters printed the same color as the paper,

words his pen uncovers one by one. It's slow going,
even with the cone of light pouring on the page
as a refrain, a trope of memory borrowed from
the extravagant fires we started with, and the figure

paused outside the window, waiting to hear his name
lifted back into life, through the sour medium
of my late-night breath. The wind in last year's leaves
sounds like static. The silence between us is complete.

The Drunk Singer (II)

Later now, in the year and in her voice,
with her band all occupied in boxing up
their dismal instruments, the sorry woods
and worn-out brasses that kept them so absorbed
three sets into the night, so she works on
her rum and Diet-Coke and pages through
the wind-swept Fake Book of her mind, as if

she still could fit the moment to its song
with such a pitchy voice, the strain of trying
to fill an empty house at closing time
bending each note a little off the mark,
while she wonders if she's *Crazy, for being
so blue*, and just *How Blue Can You Get*, before
deciding either *Too Blue* or *Almost Blue*.

And on the fogged-in highway home, the man
who's had too much is listening to the noise
of noise, the wheels-on-wet-sand sound of stations
missed, and finding that his teeth aren't sharp enough
to scrape off his tongue the taste of corn and wheat
wrung through the digestion of a Tennessee
distillery, as he moves deeper into the in-between,
this patch of low-lying November weather, and worries
at his radio, pushing all the little silver knobs
again and again and again, each effort corrected
immediately by the next, the same mistake,
the same grains of static released at every point,
until he shuts the whole thing off and hears
nothing, in its diminished form, continuing.

Photo by Catherine Foy

John Foy was born in New York City in 1960. His first book
of poetry was *Techne's Clearinghouse* (Zoo, 2005). His work has
appeared widely in magazines, including *Poetry,* the *New Yorker,*
the *New Criterion,* and *Parnassus,* and it has been featured on
the Poetry Daily website. Formerly of Bear Stearns, he now
works as a senior financial editor at Itaú USA Securities Inc.
He has spent much time in France and Brazil and now lives
in New York with his wife, son, and daughter.

Local Superstition

O my old night house.
I walk your property again
under five white stars
to see my rusted fence, my rock,
my maple tree—still there,
still chillingly legitimate.
Deer in the dark
move along the wood line
like the ghosts of débutantes
who've died violently and don't remember.

In my pocket your keys
on the galvanized ring,
hard old shiners
dying to be used.
I'm tired of their obsessive pleading.
I won't go through your doors,
afraid as I am of the dogs,
the basement. She's in there,
accusatory, sad,
sitting with her 12-gauge shotgun
and her big tin pots.

What about the analyst,
that expensive friend
who'd intercede for a fee?
What will he do with his candle,
stuck on the first step
down into your storm cellar,
a Grendel waiting for him,
prehistorically hungry?

No need to summon the professionals.
No remuneration
for hankering around the night house.
I crouch judiciously behind my rock
reciting weird Norwegian names
to drive off the doppelgänger.

Will her voice come back tonight
to this periphery?
I used to swear I'd follow her
to caves in the Carpathian Mountains,
that I'd bear up
under the rain-heavy docks of the world
like a human cantilever.
But even this last vow
has fetched up on nails.

From Rue des Martyrs

6

I wouldn't mind going crazy.
Not deeply, irrevocably mad
—just a little, enough to reach release,
to be put in hospital for awhile.
I wouldn't mind the nurses when they'd come
with warm fluids, I wouldn't mind, at night,
the orderlies in the green corridor.
I'd welcome the hours of reflection,
the time I could use to muse upon
the alarmingly infinite network
of relations and their analogies.

I'd welcome whatever came,
encourage the shy appearance
of the triangle and the clear blue sphere.

8

Coming from the bathroom at 4:00 a.m.,
hesitating by the stairs
in civilization's attic,
lightbulbs blown out long ago,
I'm braced to see what I pray I won't,
some unholy wailing raw-head
spinning itself out
from the most inhospitable part of the self
to dog the other parts to death.
Or would I see a species of angel,
something out of Botticelli
gazing preternaturally
as a mother would upon her child,
who finds you here, just where she thought you'd be?

9

The question isn't whether I see ghosts
but whether they see me,
relatives arriving blindly
from the reverse side of fact,
a bewildering trip.
They signal not the end of sanity
but the sharpening of the eye,
sanity only a clinical gauge
of the extent to which vision is impaired.
We speak fearfully, like tourists,
of "the dark place" and "the dunes of the dead,"
when we ought to speak of home,

whose terminals, alive, we are,
the ghosts coming to relieve our loneliness.

11

In holey socks and underpants
I lay on the garret floor,
closed my eyes, perspired, waited,
listening to Gregorian chants,
one high, lonely, incorporeal tenor
crystalline even on my cheap tape deck,
the rattling little piece of Sony plastic
that I used but hated.
I tried, like St. Anthony,
to ignore the cracked, plaster window frame
and the floorboards under me, refractory
and warped in that galling game,
the cenobite inside his cell
clawed by the terrestrial.

19

I look out from my weather-cracked window
at lights on the horizon at night
—a thousand propositions. Three compel the eye:
a red, blue, and green all in a line
between the Panthéon and St. Sulpice.
Luminaries keeping their distance,
three weird lithium girls
beyond time's power to dispel,
their desire safely disembodied
which otherwise could move the world.
Each night they come back glimmering
with Aristotelian clarity
—no question yet, no overture,
but already they know my name.

Techne's Clearinghouse

(George Washington Bridge, New York City)

Bridge out there in the big cold,
a bare location,
my storm-colored dominator

of ten million rivets
illumined in a nighttime
to which large things belong,

I want not just to speak to you,
but for you somehow to understand,
that I might make my way

a little less harrowingly
in the dispensation of things.
I've seen you on the long approach,

clean as a differential equation
strung between the Cloisters and the cliffs,
and I've have fallen more than half in love

with planes of shifting light,
the diamonds in the traffic's lit-up veins,
and the voice of your megalomania,

like the sound of trains,
a deep angelus going out
to all the equipment we've devised,

the F-16, the dirty winch,
the cyclohexane refinery,
and your fair sister of the other side,

thrown and fury-fused,
who knows too well this litany.
I've been too long among these things,

too quiet, objectified like them,
using *thing* to indicate
whatever does its time

in Techne's clearinghouse,
only now to find myself
inside among machinery

and fouled with distribution.
How far have we let it go,
the estrangement,

a bad marriage to utility
blinding us to higher purpose?
It's been too long,

this living, mute and paralyzed,
at the foot of buildings
as we've conceived them till now,

the windy interchangeables.
My talking to you helps allay
the fear, always with me,

that you, the sad king of induration,
may be too far gone to understand.
Lording your geometry and lights,

you're everything I've always dreamed
the mineral kingdom could become.
What am I left with

when I need to speak of you,
an angle-iron deity
of arch, thrust, interval,

too big now for the name of *thing*,
an evacuated word. Yet if any
cleated spectacle can justify

that old capacious name, it's you,
Mammon's Harp, a system
for celebrating steel

while the bells ring out in pandemonium.
There is no end
to the trouble of things,

their gravity and fatigue.
Maybe I can help you in a way,
inured as I am, all my kind,

to wandering about, trying to make do
in a blizzard of phenomena.
Susceptible as I am

to every ghost of every chance,
I know that more inheres
than the trigonometric logic

you're so terribly welded to,
my real and glittering interlocutor.
Leaving, as I must,

the fixations of the engineer,
and risking reprisal
to listen in on what goes on

way up there in the cables
and towers in the wind,
I put these words to you.

Paterfamilias

(*John C. W. Foy, 1919–1997*)

I try to think of what I'd say
were you to come back tonight,
sublunary though not
entirely terrestrial,
wanting maybe to come home
and talk about the howitzers,
the shelling, and the hail.

I know that if I tried
to reach for you, to hold you in my arms,
I'd fail the way Aeneas did
in that pathetic underworld,
where three times he tried
to apprehend what he had loved,
and the has-beens laughed by Cocytus.

Clear-headed now, with eyes rinsed out
by rain, no more the fool,
I wouldn't ask you why you'd come
or how it was contrived, though I
would tell you all about
Catherine and Christopher
—Christopher you never knew.

Terminal

What if, past a certain point, it weren't
so bad to die? What if it were like
lying on a couch at 3:00 a.m.,
the mind aloft and quiet, given over
to a few piano notes finding ways
melodically through predetermined loops
in Brian Eno's *Music for Airports?*
That's what you'd be listening to,
music for those places where we go
to go away, the music of going away,
and you just disappearing into it
without effort or pain,
finding peace in knowing *to obey*
means at its root only to listen.

Jason Gray was born in Hibbing, Minnesota, in 1976. His books include the Hollis Summers Prize–winning *Photographing Eden* (Ohio University Press, 2008) and the chapbooks *How to Paint the Savior Dead* (Kent State University Press, 2007) and *Adam & Eve Go to the Zoo* (Dream Horse, 2003). Individually, his poems and reviews have appeared in *Poetry,* the *American Poetry Review,* the *Threepenny Review,* the *Southern Review,* and elsewhere, and have earned him a grant from the Maryland State Arts Council and a Tennessee Williams Scholarship from the Sewanee Writers' Conference. Currently, he works as journals manager at the Ohio State University Press in Columbus, Ohio, and coedits the online poetry magazine *Unsplendid* (http://www.unsplendid.com).

The Snow Leopard

In the Metro Toronto Zoo

For Paul Strong

He pads on grassy banks behind a fence,
    with measured paces slow and tense.

Beyond his cage his thoughts are sharp and white;
    he lives a compelled anchorite.

A solid ghost gone blind with all the green,
    he waits and waits to be unseen.

Chiaroscuro

It's imperceptible, the line where light
Transforms to dark, or where awake becomes
Asleep, alone in the bed with dawn around
The bend of Christ's head in Caravaggio's
The Taking of Christ, hung up as a copy
Until the grime and age were cleaned away.
He's the master of *chiaroscuro*,
The slide from dark to light—this criminal,
On the run for most of his career from one
Rage or another, named in honor of
The angel Michael, brandishing a brush.
All crimes are done in dark, all crimes will meet
The light, says Christ, who suffered too at night—
The scent of anemone sent up with prayer,
The incensed guards approach in twos and then
Engulf him. The troubled sleepers raise their swords,

But in the end, who will sleep well this night?
Perhaps it's a gift for you, the long nights where
You know nothing but imponderable ache:
To be given dark, to face it when it fills
The bed, because so much will be withdrawn
From life, so much and not enough. And Christ,
Who knows the night's for kissing, pities you,
And knows the gradient you live upon.
To be given dark, the shadows on the wall
Like iron grillwork of a stair you can't
Decide to take or not, but then it's only
Gray and seamless wall. All our crimes are done
And there's the mundane miracle of the sun.

Adam & Eve Go to the Zoo

It is Adam who stops at the front gate
Even though it's open and held back.
He quivers as if he's thought of a splinter.
Eve is already looking past the iron gates
Into the plotted wilderness that aches
Inside of her like a vague déjà vu.

There is the walrus, there is the fox,
There is the panda and his hiding box.

Adam is drawn to bears: the bloated mass
Of brown fur, heavy-pawed. He feels this way:
Without dexterity. Yet Adam is
In awe of the secret nimbleness their fingers
And his contain. He wonders if someone, maybe
Even Eve, will ask to see how they work.

Eve finds herself pressed against the glass
Of the gorilla, bigger than she,
Whom she imagines she could fit inside,
The swell of child, or the ultraviolet
Blossom of soul. She hopes that maybe the bee
Will see what is beyond her vision now.

Here is the goat, here is the lamb,
Here is the camel with his head in the sand.

Here is Adam in the butterfly
Enclosure, disappointed by the silence.
Eve comes upon him here, and the monarchs come
And nest in her hair. She feels as if the wind
Has visited her; and Adam takes one on
His finger and lets Eve give it lift with breath.

The nursery, at last: egg-white and full
Of murmur; the cub is suckling milk
From a bottle; bright new sheep for the grasslands
Tumble; Adam and Eve are still at last
(Their breath marks on the glass). This is
The world that they were born for, if not born into.

Here is the woman, here is the man.
Here is the earth in the palm of our hand.

Letter to the Unconverted

And what would you say if I told you the deer had spoken?
    Two animals, we were face to face in the wood
And stopped each other dead in the last light
    Of day, the cold coming down the hillside,

Descending as ash that would preserve us like this,
　　Clay jars that could crumble at the lightest push,
Here in this moment, or the next (that haven
　　Of the already dead), crumbling in a flash

Of powder, still too late to catch the spirit
　　Escaped, wild and full of unknown sound,
Virgin language to the eager ear,
　　Beautiful unearthly distance unwound.

What would you say if I told you this? The light
　　Detached like a ghost, expanded before it broke
With bark and dirt, and watched the two of us
　　Solidify. What would you say? The deer spoke.

My Daughter as the Angel Gabriel in the Tableau Vivant of Van Grap's *Annunciation*

I gave birth to an angel, which is wrong
Twice over, though it's hard to resist the thought.
I neither gave birth to her (just ask my wife)
Nor is she an angel (just ask her rattled teacher).
And yet there she is, in white and wings,
Long lily in one hand, the other held
To Mary as God's proxy. Scrap semantics,
Embrace your sentimentality, I say,
Despite the better angels of my nature.
She is still as she never is at home.
Still enough to be one of the host.
I do not want responsibility
For words, so let my daughter be an angel,
Let the painting live as if a stone were rolled.

It is the ultimate *trompe l'oeil* on stage,
They are there, and they are not, the way
I could pull back the curtain on this sight
To show you all the brushstrokes, that the child
On stage is not my daughter, but may be
An angel yet, one of those who is there
And not there in the corners of our eyes,
Which this little play has meant to fool,
Not out of any malice for the viewer
But to make a world in which I have a daughter,
Because I wish I did, and never will.

Meditations of the Tomb Painters

I.

The pyramid has fallen in my nightmare,
And I am trapped inside of Pharaoh's tomb.
The yellow ceiling stars crashed down to earth
To the cenotaphs below. The beer jars cracked
Around his sarcophagus, ushabtis dashed
To the dust, canopic organs under stone.
The words of Osiris broken, the sun-boat scuttled,
Split entrails of Hathor are anyone's to read.
In some hard sentence on our labor, here
Are all the years of work collapsed around
The skin of god inside a scroll of linen,
Sealed from the silent, desiccated air.
A thousand nights gone by I've never had
This dream before: The king and I are dead,
With sand and rock and empire on our head.

2.

No king will cross without my services.
A recitation of the words I write
Calls the afterlife to open. My touch
Is feather-light on the glyphs whose pattern will
Be as the stones across a stream. No drop
Of water will undo his drying skin.

For practice, I paint them on my walls at home.
It is not sacred, but it hides the question
What golden boat will come for me?
The words are fog below the cliffs and I
Am quarried stone. When I die, plaster me
With papyrus reeds and leave me for the bees.

3.

We salted oil to keep down the smoke
And so there was no border between the flame
And the black air. An oval on the wall
Was all we had—a small sun where we fixed
The images for Pharaoh's passing through.
The gauze was being twisted as we worked.

And where was he now, having died and not
Yet risen, incubating, pigment mixing
With water? It is known where he will be;
I have foretold his story on the wall.
What middle country holds his soul these days,
The seventy I have to paint his world:

Here is Osiris touching Pharaoh's head;
Here is the boat across the lonely river;
Here is my heart in paint a stowaway
Inside the art that only God would see.

From The War Poems of Pope Innocent II

The Ban on Christian Burial for Those Who
Participate and Die in Jousts
Canon 14, Second Lateran Council (AD 1139)

Because it came of boasting, Innocent
II banned internment on holy grounds
   Of knights who had to prove their hands
At arms by jousting in a tournament.

They did it anyway. The metal flashed
The sun's glare back to the anxious audience—
   The gallery waited for the chance
Of disaster—this was news to be rehashed

For weeks, until the next one. The knights charged.
Dust exploded around the horses' flanks,
   The rumble shook the gallery planks.
A cracking. Brutal, swift—a quick war staged

For honor, or glory, or money, or vengeance, or
Entertainment (the town crier's lips
   Are open as the body slips
From horse to earth, but not the Church's store).

We Have Our Inheritance

At Eliot's house in Boston we kissed. I put
My fingers [Power lines crisscrossed the street]—
The tigers, restless for their sides of meat,
Stood on hind legs and peeked through the door shut
To keep them outside. This was Providence,
The Roger Williams Zoo where we first knew

There are no bars. But there are bars: a few
Words on old signs said so, and *after this*

Our exile were we inside then, or both,
Like the folded-in skin of your open mouth?
We watched the tigers ineffectually scratch
The trees, each swipe sounding like a clicking latch.
—[made a net for the sky] on your buttons, but,
Touching the house, you sighed, the way was shut.

GEORGE GREEN

Photo by Giordani

George Green was born in Grove City, Pennsylvania, in 1950. He received an MFA in poetry from the New School and currently teaches at Lehman College, CUNY, in the Bronx. His poems have appeared in the anthologies *Poetry 180, 180 More,* and *The Best American Poetry 2005* and *2006*.

The Death of Winckelmann

Trieste 1768

I.

The Abbé Winckelmann was at his desk
in the hotel, when his new friend Francesco
returned, ostensibly in search of his
dropped handkerchief. He asked to see, once more,
the special medals from Her Holy Empress,
and Winckelmann obliged him merrily
by waving them like censers in the air.
Done with his "fair Antinous" charade,
Francesco made his move and pulled a knife,
intent on robbery. A fight ensued,
and Winckelmann was stabbed at least five times.
Some servant, hearing cries, surprised the thief,
who fled, with gory hands, into the street
and hid himself nearby inside a shed.
The Abbé staggered to the balcony,
pressing a cloth against his streaming wounds.

II.

He'd argued that the turbulent Laocoön
embodied chaste decorum and restraint.
Sedateness was a virtue in itself,
for this bookish son of an epileptic cobbler.
Gripping the banister, he had become
a grisly simulacrum of the statue,
peering in desperation, faintly, down
into the dim and cavernous hotel.
A bustling group of servants mounted toward

him on the stairs, some shrieking in their panic,
until they reached him finally and hushed,
stopping to catch their breath before they tipped
him gently down onto a mattress. Then,
as though he truly were a wounded king
or holy martyr, some fell on their knees,
while some like saints or ancient Romans stood
and hid their pallid faces in their hands.

III.

Poor Winckelmann had met his murderer
only the week before. Francesco heard
him asking about ships, and, butting in,
told Winckelmann that he knew of a captain
whose brigantine was ready to embark.
The two men set out for the quay but went
instead to a coffeehouse where both indulged
forbidden inclinations. They returned
to the hotel and were inseparable
thereafter, although both were unforthcoming.
The Abbé served as Papal Antiquary
and never told his friend. Francesco failed,
for his part, to disclose that he had just
been freed from jail. He thought the Abbé was
a spy or an adventurer, perhaps
a Lutheran or a Jew. At any rate,
there by himself, with money, in Trieste,
he made an easy mark for young Francesco.
The scholar had been frantic to persuade
his *amoroso* to return with him
and foolishly showed off a golden snuffbox,
a gift from the Marquis of Tavistock.

IV.

He'd hoped to die held in the broken arms
of his beloved Apollo Belvedere
and glide through heaven pressed to that pure stone.
But now a guardsman thumbed his battered *Iliad*,
while a condoling monk assisted him
in drawing up a will, which he would die
trying to sign. Francesco, on the wheel,
would bawl and beg for death, then lie exposed
as fare for famished dogs and harbor fowl.
A courier, dispatched to Rome, would bring
the awful tidings to the Vatican.
Cassandra-like, Frau Kaufmann went to Mass,
and, trudging through the galleries, distraught,
Mengs wept before the Barberini Faun.
The medals were discovered by a cardinal,
uncatalogued, among the Abbé's things.

V.

We have our own Apollo Belvedere,
which Winckelmann inspired, at the Met.
A grand Canova on the balcony,
of Perseus rampant with the baleful head.
The victor with his magic shoes and helmet
is otherwise stark naked in the court
of Polydectes, where he hoists his trophy,
high and dripping, up before the hall,
to petrify the whole licentious rout
and end the tyrant's terrible misrule.
The scene, at last, was what the gods had wished.
Our hero rode through town, pelted with flowers,
while pageants overspread the countryside.

Danaë rejoiced, the Nereids rejoiced,
Andromeda rejoiced in broken chains,
for Perseus had delivered up the palace
and greeted faithful Dictus with the crown.

My Uncle's Bible

The pastel maps that show the Holy Land
are dimmer now. This rubber band is all
that holds the prophets back, who otherwise
flop out and sprawl along the floor like clowns.
My uncle was a navigator, killed
above the clouds, and when they mailed it back
with silver cufflinks and a wrinkled tie,

its binding was already torn and loose.
Had it been shot down too? My Grandma wondered.
She wasn't in the mood for metaphors.
Maybe my uncle damaged it himself;
he couldn't take it, not another raid
and, furious with terror, chucked his Bible,
cracking its spine against the barracks wall.

It may be time for me to chuck it too.
It's moldering. On somber days it looks
like it was wrested from a lunatic
or lodged by a tornado in a tree.
What could I swear to on its rotten hide?
This Good Book, yearning for oblivion,
the dump its long-awaited Kingdom Come.

Warhol's Portraits

Liz

Marilyn killed herself because she thought
that middle age began at thirty-five.
In Liz's case it did, but she kept going,
though Dick went down in flames (*Exorcist II*).
This print's from '65 and she looks ready
to frug the night away with Peter Lawford,
who hasn't started wearing beads (not yet).
Those were the days, before the TV movies,
before the Percocet and Häagen-Dazs.
Oblivious to the telltale signs, she smiles,
the long descent to Neverland begun.

Mick Jagger

He is in my opinion past his prime
already in this print, and he and Keith
are fast becoming tacky little skanks
and sherry-slurping, chicken-headed whores.
They shake their butts and sweat in leather pants,
like ancient drag queens high on Angel dust.

Dennis Hopper

His cowboy Hamlet death scenes are the best.
He flops, jerks, and blabs beseechingly,
then flops, imploringly, and dies. John Wayne,
even, is stunned by so much hamminess.
(He kills him twice: *True Grit* and *Katie Elder*).
Now Dennis sells investments on TV,
blabbing away to boomers who have bucks

enough to golf all day, enough to die
of boredom in the sun. Dennis is cool, though,
and still the hippest actor on the scene.
A poet and a painter, and, what's more,
a recognized authority on Andy.

Goethe

From Tischbein's portrait of the noble poet
lounging beside a shattered obelisk.
The campiness of Goethe's hat and cloak
no doubt explains why Andy did this copy.
The coloring is pure Electric Circus
and Maharishi-era Donovan.
"The savoring of unintended ironies"
is Peter Schjeldahl in last week's *New Yorker*
explaining camp to dopes out in the burbs.

Deborah Harry

She is expressionless, or nearly so,
and yet the muffled insolence is there,
a look that prom queens have—the secret stoners;
a look that cover girls will overdo.
I've seen that look on Bombay prostitutes
in coffee-table books, but, some of them,
pathetically, look out at us with hope,
as if a photograph could rescue them
or set them up inside a better cathouse.

Truman Capote

Those A-list types who had rejected Andy
(Capote, Rauschenberg, and Jasper Johns)
all came around when he got really big,

though friendship had become extraneous.
The portraits of his friends are extra flat.
You can't look into them: There is no in.
A frightful vacancy and transience
is what, I guess, he meant us all to see.
He might as well have kept on painting shoes.

Jerry Hall

I could step back and make a case for these,
regard them, somehow, in another light.
Maybe the sitters have been divinized
and that's why they all fade into abstraction.
Maybe those patches where the colors smear,
blurring the lines, express the soul's diffuse
ethereality, reminding us
of what, time and again, the Lord enjoins—
that we behold each other as divine.

Mao

The Chairman's constipation was so bad,
he only defecated once a week,
and during the Long March his weekly voidings
were sometimes celebrated by his troops.
Mao moved his bowels once on a mountaintop
above the clouds, and members of his staff
began to dance and clap their hands. The news
spread rapidly as cheers went up along
the mountain side. The tattered ranks rejoiced,
ten thousand hats were tossed into the air!
From goat trails near the summit bugles sounded,
and acclamations echoed in the dells.

Stephen Duck and Edward Chicken

failed to make it into Schmidt's *Lives of the Poets*.
Duck, "The Thresher Poet of Pewsey Downs,"
would vault into the court of Caroline
and marry Sarah Big, her housekeeper.
"The Muse's Darling, Reverend Duck is dead,"
wrote Mary Collier, "The Poetical Washer-Woman,"
upon the unhappy event.
Also lamenting Duck were Henry Jones,
"The Poetical Bricklayer," and "Lactilla,
The Poetical Milkmaid of Clifton Hill."
Lactilla later wrote *The Royal Captives*,
an elephantine novel in five volumes,
which kept the wistful milkmaid at her desk
like a galley slave chained drooping to an oar.

I'd like to tell you more but Southey's splendid
Lives of the Uneducated Poets
is unavailable today from Bobst Library.
He made his pile off Valium, Elmer Bobst,
and that's just fine with me.
A Valium might have rescued Reverend Duck,
who drowned himself, Lord help us,
in a pond behind a rowdy, rustic tavern.
And while we're at it, pass the Valium, please,
to John Gould Fletcher (decades out of print),
who won the Pulitzer in '39,
drowned himself in a murky Ozark duck pond,
and failed, likewise, to make it into Schmidt.
He was rich, I think. Chicken was maybe a curate.

"The Poetical Bag-lady of Astor Place"
boards the 6 train and curses the entire car
for being "illiterate." "Spell mayonnaise,"
she hollers in my face. "Spell mayonnaise!"
And, discombobulated, I cannot.

JOSEPH HARRISON

Joseph Harrison was born in Richmond, Virginia, in 1957.
His books of poetry are *Someone Else's Name* (Waywiser,
2003) and *Identity Theft* (Waywiser, 2008). His poems are
anthologized in the Library of America's *American Religious
Poems*, *180 More: Extraordinary Poems for Every Day*, *The Best
American Poetry 1998*, and *The New Penguin Pocket Anthology
of Poetry*. *Someone Else's Name* was a finalist for the Poets'
Prize and was chosen one of five poetry books of the year
for 2004 by the *Washington Post*. In 2005 Joseph Harrison
won an Academy Award in Literature from the American
Academy of Arts and Letters. An associate editor of the
Waywiser Press, he lives in Baltimore.

Nautical Terms

"Words alone are certain good."

Not all that long ago,
We were nautical folk: barges and sloops,
    Clippers and steamers and sharpies,
Were how we got wherever we had to go,
        Moved goods and troops
        Or fled Virgilian harpies,
As if all destinations were the slips
    Where we could dock our ships.

That's changed, of course: sports car
And jumbo jet, r. v. and high-speed train,
    Aiming at stations, lots,
And carpeted ports, carry us near and far
        Through wind and rain
        To plush vacation spots
Which proffer heated pools and personal trainers.
    Now ships are for containers.

But as we moved on we
Carried the signs of our seafaring phases
    Embedded in language itself.
We glide like shadows miles above the sea,
        But common phrases
        Accrete like an ocean shelf,
Layer on layer, sedimental, slow,
    To tell more than we know.

For did we *know the ropes*,
We'd hear the echoes of maritime concerns

Haunting the current cline,
Like sextants, compasses, and telescopes
    Guiding our turns
    Of phrase: we *toe the line,*
End up *over the barrel,* or get *dressed down*
    Lest we screw up and drown.

Old senses linger, whether
We're stuck *in the doldrums* like a floating jail
    Or *buoyed up.* We say,
Without much thought, that we're *under the weather.*
    Dark skies prevail,
    Then there's *the devil to pay:*
Like waves, old moods well up and *overwhelm*
    The logic *at the helm.*

Then, to escape our funk,
We *tie one on,* and, *three sheets to the wind,*
    We wind up *in the head*
Or *over the rail,* groggy, falling-down drunk.
    We're caught, we're ginned
    (We'd be better off dead)
Between the devil and the deep blue sea,
    Footloose, not fancy free.

Since cautionary tales
Abound, like perils, on the salty freeway,
    The sea's our strategic crib.
No great shakes? Take the wind out of his sails.
    He warrants *leeway?*
    Noting *the cut of his jib*
We *give a wide berth* to the *son of a gun,*
    With room to *cut and run.*

Though context, *by and large,*
Has *gone by the board,* language doesn't *start*
Over with a clean slate.
Words get *pressed into service,* with a charge
That's worlds apart.
At *the bitter end* it's late,
We've garbled it all, not knowing, our *logbooks* shut,
The linguistic *scuttlebutt.*

How many years before
Our most precise locutions, our most fine
Inflections and gradations
Of subtle sense, mean nothing anymore,
Dead on the line?
What unforeseen mutations
Will wrench our phrases, context overthrown,
Particulars unknown?

A cautionary tale:
Like Corinth, Babylon, and Jericho
Splintered to shards and scraps,
So too such terms. They're terminal. Detail
Will blur and go.
Philologists, perhaps,
Will piece together something of the past
We were, who did not last.

Way back when we were young
We clambered up the rigging. At full sail,
We flew. Who could misread,
Or "the mysmetre for defaute of tonge"?
How could words fail?
They're all we have, indeed.

We had not sung so surely had we known
They'd soon be on their own.

Variation on a Theme by the Weather

On the radio today they estimated
The chance of rain at one hundred percent,
    Which seems exaggerated
Given a world where chance outruns prediction
And every day some unforetold event
    Proves certainty a fiction,

Where walls that severed continents collapse
Not from the exercise of stockpiled might,
    But through the gradual lapse
Of purpose in the fabricated state
That can't get elemental functions right,
    And history can't wait,

Where favorites blow overwhelming leads,
And politicians who are on the take
    Do civic-minded deeds,
Where patients terminally ill survive,
And under the rubble of a huge earthquake
    One child is found alive,

And the most watched of variable things
Is weather which is mostly unforeseeable,
    A flow of moods and swings
That parades its perfect days, then flaunts its flaws,
Lurching from mild to disagreeable
    In sync with unruly laws

To form incalculable permutations,
Fractal patterns rippling outward through
        So many iterations
That our precise computers merely show,
For all we know now that we never knew,
        Chance limits what we know.

Yet given a swerving universe where pure
Uncertainty extends so vast a rule
        That nothing else seems sure,
In this particular case I do know how
One might say, without sounding like a fool,
        It's going to rain: it's raining now.

From the Songbook of Henri Provence

1

Arrival of the insects, and the green
        Protrusions of renewal,
As light turns on a switch and the whole scene
        Springs back to life, and all
That world of ice and snow, austere, pristine,
        And hard as any jewel,
Seems nothing now, melted to having been
        And farther off than fall.

2

The thick and sweaty air, the pounding sun,
        The miasmal steam that rises
From asphalt, track and pasture, overcome
        The simplest exercises,
Leaving us flopped on couches, listless, numb,

And stunned that spring's surprises,
The miracles we numbered one by one,
Led to such strict assizes.

3

The whirligig of leaves, the sick-sweet scent
Of fallen apples rotting,
The swift encroachment of the sun's descent
On afternoons, the plotting
Of store and pantry shelves, crammed with intent,
The Vs of geese, the nutting,
Make us forget those months that seemed hell-sent
As if their trials were nothing.

4

And now the world's a blank page, frozen hard
As disbelief, extreme
As absence, blanketing the small back yard
In flash and fitful gleam,
Concealing the cold earth we worked and scarred
Till harvest comes to seem
A distant pageant in which we humans starred
Only in some dim dream.

The Eccentric Traveler

Nature alone is perfect. In the woods
The angles of the light, crisscrossing the pines,
Portion the forest air into luminous panes
Fractured by towering shafts, and the upper boughs
Display the various tints and shades of green
Scrawled by the vines and bushes and small trees

Swarming the forest floor. All's a green blur,
And rippling through the green is a wave of song
Cresting above you, whistles and chirps and trills
Which cross and quarrel, counter and amplify,
A flowing over, spontaneous, carefree,
Implying all the purity of joy.
Then silence. Shadows alternate with sun.

Soon, in the failing light, the path begins
To grow increasingly dim, ambiguous turns
Lead nowhere fast, a path does re-emerge
But it too wanders off among the trees
And peters out. Now it is really dark,
And you have to admit you're lost, lost in the woods.
The dark is alive: it hums and crawls and watches.
You are surrounded by something extremely old
And very clearly have no business here,
Pierced by the sight-lines of a thousand eyes.
You remember all the weird stories you've heard
Of hikers who got lost around these parts,
The hippie couple on their honeymoon,
The scout who wandered from his troop, the hunter
Boastful of plans to track the local lion,
The eccentric traveler who carried bagpipes.
The wood maintains its silence on them all,
As on all those who came with the idea
That nature mirrors the best parts of us,
Inspires and elevates the human soul,
But found, in the end, whatever else they found,
Something indifferent, and only true to itself.

Even if one returns from this experience
One does so dazed, not so much disillusioned

As seeing all perception as illusion,
Like someone leaving a cave, or like, perhaps,
Someone who dies for a moment, then is revived
By science or a miracle of art,
Or like the young man out in Washington
Camping alone for the first time, a rite
Of passage into manhood, as he saw it,
Who wandered from his camp looking for water
And lost his way in the coniferous forest:
For days he wandered the primeval forest,
Eating peanut shells, then eating nothing,
And heard, again and again, the absolute silence
Of the great emerald trees silently standing
Straight up the sides of the long-standing mountains,
Then heard a raven, hoarse and raucous, caw,
Or, puncturing the air like a machine gun,
The *rat-a-tat, rat-a-tat, rat-a-tat, rat-a-tat-tat*
Of a woodpecker drilling a hollow pine,
And then the sounds would stop, as in a dream,
As on the forest went, and on he went,
Endlessly lost in the unending forest,
And dizzy from hunger, weakening from hunger,
Drifting into delirium he heard
Something that sounded very much like music
Float through the forest, as if the air were music,
Not like the song of the birds, a human music,
Moody, solitary, elegiac,
The keening, ceremonial tones of bagpipes
Crying for something lost, for someone lost,
Then, quickly, flutes encouraging the bagpipes
Into a marching ditty, and followed the music
Past the erroneous turns of the dark forest
And all the way to the Elkhorn Ranger Station,

Where, walking into their camp like an apparition,
He startled a discouraged group of searchers
(None of whom played the flute, or carried bagpipes),
Who led him, without music, out of the woods.

To My Friends

My good friends, when you're under the illusion
That the common end of things has ended me,
Whether that end was sudden or wretchedly slow,
Peaceful or violent, untimely or, finally, wished for,

Don't spend too much time grieving, as if I were gone
To some murky underground region of swampy water
And cavernous absence, metallic and silent and cold,
Or some plush resort in the stratosphere of our dreams

Pillowed with cumuli, graced by ethereal muzak,
Or some massive confusing impersonal processing center
With lines and obscure snafus and numbers not names,
Away from the sun and the sound of the wind in the trees,

But after a short ceremony, public or private,
Listen for the wings of the birds, and ask where we're going,
Alabama or Delaware, Canada, Yucatan,
And wish me luck in the next life, who now have wings.

ERNEST HILBERT

Ernest Hilbert was born in Philadelphia, Pennsylvania, in 1970. He is the author of the collection *Sixty Sonnets* (Red Hen, 2009). He was educated at Oxford University, where he studied with Jon Stallworthy and James Fenton, and edited the *Oxford Quarterly*. Upon his return to America, he became the poetry editor for Random House's magazine *Bold Type* in New York City (1999–2003) and later served as editor of the *Contemporary Poetry Review* (2005–9). He works as an antiquarian book dealer in Philadelphia, where he lives with his wife, a classical archaeologist.

Domestic Situation

Maybe you've heard about this. Maybe not.
A man came home and chucked his girlfriend's cat
In the wood chipper. This really happened.
Dinner wasn't ready on time. A lot
Of other little things went wrong. He spat
On her father, who came out when he learned
About it. He also broke her pinky,
Stole her checks, and got her sister pregnant.
But she stood by him, stood strong, through it all,
Because she loved him. She loved him, you see.
She actually said that, and then she went
And married him. She felt some unique call.
Don't try to understand what another
Person means by love. Don't even bother.

Magnificent Frigatebird

The sharp dark thorn plummets like a dive-bomber,
No human moment of hesitation
In its rush through raw wind to join its goal.
Fish gather in quick, silver clouds, swell, veer.
They swim beneath this black-lit beacon,
Long-beaked chevron of darkness, lance of coal,
Swiftly struck ink dash, aiming down hard
Like a stealth fighter, so fast it suffers
No lapse of purpose. Poised and sinister,
Over a glistening sea, the Pirate Bird
Studies the breakers for new kills, hovers—
Earth its vast blank canvas and theater—

Supreme as midday sun, brutal as the sea,
And chosen, death's fond emissary.

Mirage

Once, when I was young, an odd thing occurred.
I found myself in trouble for some stunt,
Some selfish offense forgotten since then.
For a time, my mother's smile was deferred,
And I learned it was something I would want
To get back so I could feel fine again.
For a brief but blurred flash, from the top stair,
I thought she smiled at me. What a relief.
I smiled back, but she scowled. What went wrong?
I grew confused. I was struck, standing there.
What slipped in my reckless reach for reprieve?
I grasped a mirage, unreal as a song.
I was shocked by the sheer drop from assurance,
The vast span that parts us from our parents.

Church Street

For Daniel Nester

My friends quietly dropped out of high school.
It seemed each week we had parties for some guy
Going into jail or getting released.
It's not that anyone thought this was cool,
Only good wishes that the time would fly,
And after twenty beers he might find some peace.
Now that I look back, with no emotion,

We needed parties. We liked company.
We hardly needed a reason at all:
Never sweet-sixteen or graduation,
But funeral, fresh hitch in the army,
Baby soon for the sad girl in the hall.
We'd vent, catch any reason to not grieve,
Revel down days torn from the years we'd leave.

Fortunate Ones

You will inherit large sums of money
(But someone dear to you will have to die first).
You will travel far and see the wide world
(And load yourself with debt; these things aren't free).
You can relax now. You've been through the worst
(But it consumed your youth, and now you're old).
You will enjoy many warm times with friends
(But they will sneak your booze and filch your smokes).
Your fortune is in some other cookie
(Hard to argue the message that one sends).
You are very important to your folks
(They will never let your life be easy).
A fortune is only worth what it covers
(Believe what you like, discard the others).

In Bed for a Week

It happens to us all, at least one time,
The black, caught knot of storm threatens, distant,
But buckling closer, waves capped and blown white.
Heavy tides, laden with fresh wreckage, climb,
Drop down the throat; life is a persistent

Ache of sunken vessels and squandered light.
Barrier islands and breakwaters lost,
The sea flails the darkness, its frayed currents,
Wind-flung sediment, shards like stones thrown,
Pooled mirrors blown to blur down the cold coast,
Leaving foam, crushed scum, marsh sun, a grim sense
Of many inherited contours gone.
But the dark flush in the heart will subside,
Drain slowly, slowly draw back as a tide.

Ashore

The harpooned great white shark heaves onto sand,
Nudged by waves, red cavern of dripping teeth.
A crowd comes. Loud gulls wreathe the booming mist.
Blue flies cloud the fishy sunset, and land.
One, sated, is slapped to a smear beneath
A child's quick hand and then flicked from his wrist.
Compass and munitions are sunk with skulls
In wrecks beneath old storms, glass angels
And hourglasses, flint of sunlight through motes,
Violence of slit sails, drowned crews, split hulls,
Quiet draw of dust, too, and all that it pulls,
The slow leak and loss of each thing that floats—
Flail and wild eye, flecked spit of crippled horse,
Crust of diamonds on the throat of a corpse.

All of You on the Good Earth

For Henry Wessells

Even sci-fi gurus sometimes stumble.
Some small, seemingly obvious details

Fail to fit into farsighted novels.
Robots built to be human still fumble
With decks of punch cards for brains. Other tales
Use cassette tapes to achieve time travel.
Clerks bang on typewriters beyond the last star.
Beehives and bellbottoms always stay in style.
The milkman still makes rounds, but he's a clone.
A hero, fleeing in a hover car,
Slowly spins away on a rotary dial
To activate the 3-D videophone.
A lone man emerges from a structure.
He keys a code, and turns from the locked door.

Pirates

For Jennifer Makowsky

Impatiently polite, imperious,
Our neighbors only just tolerated
The peculiar clan at cul-de-sac's end.
We were insufficiently industrious
With lawn care, and our plot was at last rated
An eyesore. How, they wondered, could we spend
So much time sleeping, so little weeding:
Crabgrass spiked brown, dandelions spackled gold.
Of an old German barbarian born,
A sour, thin kid, moping, slouching, reading,
I'd gather bruised windfall apples and throw
Them over the hedge—broadside launched with scorn
From our blue-shingled brigantine, square prow
Lodged in high grass, underneath long boughs.

Photo by Don Pollard

Adam Kirsch was born in Los Angeles in 1976. He is the
author of two collections of poems, *The Thousand Wells*
(Ivan R. Dee, 2002), winner of the New Criterion Poetry
Prize, and *Invasions* (Ivan R. Dee, 2008); two books of
criticism, *The Wounded Surgeon: Confession and Transforma-
tion in Six American Poets* (Norton, 2005) and *The Modern
Element: Essays on Contemporary Poetry* (Norton, 2008); and
a biography, *Benjamin Disraeli* (Random House, 2008). He
is a senior editor at the *New Republic*, and his essays and
reviews have appeared in the *New Yorker*, *Poetry*, and other
publications. He lives in New York City with his wife,
Remy, and his son, Charles.

The tin balls that the Planetarium
Displays to demonstrate the powers of ten
Range from the pebbly fraction of an atom
To a hot air balloon that means the sun,
Indicting cosmologically provincial
Habits they can't help but reinforce
By tailoring their exponential spiral
To the perspective of an audience
Whose unraised power is thereby made to seem
The integer of all created things.
Where is the diorama that could shame
And reconcile a creature that belongs
In the dark bowel of the universe
Only as our insides accommodate
Weird flora whose unconscious processes
We never see and couldn't live without?

From The Consolations

III.7 *Habet hoc voluptas omnis*

First the hypnosis
As the hive buzzes,
Issuing dank and honeyed promises;

Lust for the rose-
Gold-tinted ooze
Makes you forget the swarm, the sting, the bruise.

II.4 *Quisquis volet perennem*

The man who cannot hope to own
A house unless he takes a loan

He'll still be paying off when he
Is on Social Security
Might daydream of a terraced perch
On Venice or Miami Beach,
Watching the wave that scours and breaks
In sizzling phosphorescent flakes,
Swimming naked in a balmy
California January,
Breathing Floridian perfume
Of sunscreen, alcohol and brine;
But then, remembering the jolt
Preparing in the coastal fault,
The timber-smashing wind and rain
Of yearly Force Five hurricanes,
He thinks it wiser to invest
In the dry, steady, flat Midwest,
Where a small plot of solid ground
Won't lift you up or let you down.
So when the great catastrophe
Arrives, he'll watch it on TV,
See pixilated fire or flood
Destroy his almost-neighborhood,
And piously reiterate
His law of life and real estate:
The best investment's one that earns
Small but reliable returns.

V.3 *Quaenam discors foedera rerum*

Something is missing. When the telescope
Anxiously scans a sector of the night,
The numbers streaming in do not add up;
The universe would be too cold or hot,
Too dense or empty, if it weren't for

Dimensions that won't let themselves be caught.
Why is it that this absence reassures?
Dividing what we know by what we see,
We always find that permanent remainder,
The margin of an old perplexity
Now justified and even rational;
For somewhere, it is certain, there must be
The light, remembered, hypothetical,
That once made our dark matter visible.

The long, squat, leaden-windowed, burrow-like
Offices terracing the Palisades
Seem the earliest architecture, such as make
On Afghan mountains bomb-proof barricades—
Or anywhere a Third World tenantry
Survives our televised annihilation
By clamping down and taking root. To see
On the Hudson echoes of that habitation
Once could provoke humility, the theme
For abstract reveries that all is flux.
Staring across the river now, it seems
A sign of how civilization self-destructs:
Their single-minded virtuous contempt,
Our bashful Alexandrian tolerance,
Our glass towers and their common, huddling, cramped,
Impregnable cliffside. We don't stand a chance.

Calmly, the papers calculate the chance
That in ten years the planet and a shard
Of rock will consummate the long romance

We've led with ruin. This will be ignored:
Not for the small but lotto-beating odds,
But from the madman's counterfactual ease
That fissions us as always into gods
Who count in aeons and eternities,
And beasts who scavenge for the daily kill,
Gobbling down the meat that will not keep.
Does the beast suspect that nuclear winter will
Be secretly welcome as untroubled sleep,
And does the god observe the sky in peace
Since his life neither starts nor ends in weather?
Both let what will come come; for the decrees
Of the asteroid are righteous altogether.

Heroes Have the Whole Earth for Their Tomb

Tonight I read of an ancient war
Once thought self-evidently great,
Out-blazoning all that came before,
Each battlefield a hinge of fate,

And marvel once more at how the gain
Or loss of some extinguished city
Could cause defeated men such pain
And win for the conqueror such glory.

Who wondered then if Amphipolis
Merited agonizing death,
Or doubted that mighty Brasidas
Would, for as long as men drew breath,

Shine forth in his dear-bought renown?
And when did the majesty of act

Imperceptibly dwindle down
To indifferent, objective fact?

Athens and Sparta gripped each other
For thirty years; all those who died
Piled in a single trench together
Could not for an hour have pacified

Insatiable Passchendaele; the dead
Rise in an exponential series
From units in the Megarid
Up to the hundred thousand bodies

Now nourishing the green Ardennes.
If trophies were to be built for all,
The urns would leave no room for men,
The names would require an endless wall.

History that the Greeks released,
Unconscious of evil, from the lamp,
Now finds its scale so far increased
That atom-bomb and murder-camp

Draw less profusion from the heart
Than a few soldiers killed at sea
When Pericles, in the crowded mart,
Read out his invented eulogy.

A Love Letter

First, the preliminaries. Let me tell
Why I will try to say these things in verse,

Which I know by experience is hardly well
Suited to heartfelt explanation; worse,
In an awkward stanza, one that cannot dwell
On a subject patiently, but must reverse
Its train of thought and mine, so that I move
Only haltingly to the final station, love.

Maybe I need exactly that impediment,
Though everyone knows that speaking from the heart
Should be like a river, onrushing, with sediment
(In this case, natural clumsy words) the part
That, caught up, proves its force; then what I said I meant
Could not be doubted as a trick of art,
But, like the stream that past its channel flows,
Would prove its sincerity by turning prose.

How natural just to speak; our situation
Is a common one (though we're fortunate to get it)
And doesn't require such willful complication,
Which cannot illuminate, but may upset it;
Better to try the three-word declaration
That could summarize all mine, if I would let it;
It's not as clever, but it still might move you
If instead of this I simply wrote "I love you."

But, like a Bible text, that simple phrase
Contains enough matter for a page of glosses;
As a slide, which to the naked eye displays
A point, in the microscope is a colossus,
It appears to mean precisely what it says,
But read as we read it, the expression loses
All obvious meaning, so that when we're through
We can't be sure of "I" or "love" or "you."

The middle term, which seems the most abstract,
Is the least confusing. It is what remains,
The one irrefutable, all-enduring fact,
Through a thousand ruptures, petty shocks and strains
That can only momentarily distract,
But never part us; love waxes and wanes,
But, like the hide-and-go-seek of the moon,
It is only hiding, never really gone.

The problem—or, since it need not be solved,
The mystery—is not love but the lover;
Us, the two pronouns so deeply involved
In the transitive verb. For I cannot discover
The element in me that is not dissolved
By a change of time or place; the days are over
When I thought that attaching to my name
Was a portable essence, everywhere the same.

Think of that spring, the strange inauguration
Of the reign in which we are still living now
(Though there were interregnums, an occupation
By a foreign power). We watched the river flow
Flashingly past us, and its mute elation
Gave me the courage (still I don't know how)
To say what my odd behavior had implied,
To ask what I thought could not have been denied.

Said what? Asked what? And has it been five years
Since that first embrace, unlooked for, wild, momentous?
The river still flows, still flashes, and still hears
From new undergraduate lips the old portentous
Soft declarations; all the world appears
To them as it did to us; their own tremendous

Hour, the one that realigns their fate,
Could be now, this day their secret, holy date.

But we cannot step again in that same river;
It has flowed past us, though it has remained
In the same course, and will remain forever
(Or at least till the city's engineers have trained
Its floods into some more practical endeavor);
For the lives we had then cannot be regained.
Today is for hypothetical new lovers,
And tomorrow their rapture also will be over.

That night we were pledged (not quite explicitly)
To love and each other. But if we have moved
So far from that spot, that life, are we implicitly
Freed from the promise our old selves approved?
Couldn't we say the contract was illicitly
Signed by two strangers, who that night had loved,
Using our names, their now-heirs and assigns
Who are slaves to their tyrannical designs?

Or say, if that seems too much exaggeration,
We are like the ship that, in the story, sailed
To a hundred ports, and at each destination
Took on new masts in place of those that failed,
Until, in the course of a ten-year navigation,
Each plank was changed; was the ship that came
To the isle it departed different or the same?

And yet we fare forward. How? Look at the way
We talk about love, to the words that do not lie;
Proclaiming it to the world we do not say
"I love," as though love depended on the I

Whose resolves can be altered twenty times a day,
But rather "I am in love," and so imply
That love, like a necessary atmosphere,
Surrounds us, pure or polluted, everywhere.

Love is a faith, though not because the lover
Sees a divinity in his darling's eyes
(Love made on that principle would soon be over,
Unless, as with Beatrice, she quickly dies);
But love becomes for him the Unmoved Mover
No logical proof explains or justifies;
He rejoices that in love at last he's found
The self-evident good, the all-sustaining ground.

Dearest, though it's taken me so long
To reach the point where I openly address you,
I already fear I've written this all wrong,
Said something unwittingly that may distress you.
If you've found anything here that's true or strong,
Your presence made it so; but I confess, you
Will be justified if you are only critical,
Since all my powers, poetic, analytical,

Cannot do justice to the theme. You are
The atmosphere, the river, and the ground,
The ship, the destiny, and many more
Mysterious things for which I haven't found
Appropriate or becoming metaphors:
For a word, we've learned, is an arbitrary sound
Yoked to a meaning, and will never do
To describe what's essential, necessary, true.

So no more words. Already it is late,
And soon it will be night, and time for sleeping;

A thousand miles of darkness separate
My bed from yours, but let there be no weeping;
Time parted us, but I believe that fate
Will deliver you somehow to my safekeeping,
And trust, what is impossible to prove,
That all will be well with us and with our love.

JOANIE MACKOWSKI

Photo by Charlie Green

Joanie Mackowski, born in Illinois in 1963, has lived in
eight states and on three coasts. *View from a Temporary
Window*, her second book of poetry, will be available from
the Pitt Poetry Series late in 2009; her book *The Zoo* (Pitt
Poetry Series, 2002) was awarded the AWP Award Series
in Poetry and the Kate Tufts Discovery Award. Formerly a
Wallace Stegner Fellow at Stanford University and a Rona
Jaffe Fellow, Mackowski teaches in the Creative Writing
Program at the University of Cincinnati, and she has also
worked as a journalist, a translator, and a juggler.

Portrait

Is there nowhere to turn? So the chair isn't stable,
and storm clouds drift through the glass table.
It's been a hard day. You're dying for dinner.
Perhaps your own body sat down too near you,

or are you in love? With a song, for an hour,
or with the one clean break you press to your core?
Why else does the span of your arms reach so wide:
one hand touches summer, the other's got winter.

What can you do? Fold swans on the pond,
the moon on your thumb—and now you bend
down to straighten the lamplight's odd patterns.
When you take off your shirt, is the sun among the buttons,

red-orange, setting, draped over the chair?
And when the sun rises, when it paints your picture
in pink and blue on the wall by the bed,
does its love for your faults make you feel any better?

And your shadow is wrong. It weighs too large,
bends too easy, slipping over each edge
of the table, its dark accordion singing down the stairs.
But the larkspur in the meadow is the shadow of the stars

as evening descends. More stars start hatching,
caught in the treetops, scratching your chin.
Are you running from someone, tired of the sky,
the last light wedged over the trees like a scar;

have you twisted him together with feathers and twine?
The quiet pond nestles in the crook of your arm.

You feel uneven, but there's no one to blame,
and evening waits at your lips like a plum.

Larger

I don't know how it happened, but I fell—
and I was immense, one dislocated arm
wedged between two houses. I felt some ribs
had broken, perhaps a broken neck, too;
I couldn't speak. My dress caught bunched about
my thighs and where my glasses shattered there spread
a seacoast; where my hair tangled with power lines
I felt a hot puddle of blood.

                      I must have passed out,
for when I woke, a crew of about fifty
was winding stairway beside my breast
and buttressing a platform on my sternum.
I heard, as through cotton, the noise of hammers,
circular saws, laughter, and some radio
droning songs about love. Some ate their lunch
on a hill of black cypress, all blurry; from the corner
of one eye I saw my pocketbook, its contents
scattered, my lipstick's toppled silo glinting
out of reach. And then, waving a tiny flashlight,
a man entered my ear. I felt his boots sloshing
the fluid trickling there. He never came out.
So others went looking, with flares, dogs, dynamite
even: they burst my middle ear and found
my skull, its cavern crammed with dark matter
like a cross between a fungus and a cloud.
They never found his body, though.

                      Now my legs subdue
that dangerous sea, the water bright enough

to cut the skin, where a lighthouse, perched on the tip
of my great toe, each eight seconds rolls
another flawless pearl across the waves.
It keeps most ships from wrecking against my feet.
On clear days, people stand beside the light;
they watch the waves' blue heads slip up and down
and scan for landmarks on the facing shore.

Under the Shadow

A silverfish on my pillow, dropping off into a box
of books, a fruit fly hovering, and sow bugs,

cousin to the barnacle: seven dead curled
beneath the tub (held to the light, they're gold);

one live one, all perfect articulation and large
as a tooth, easing around the edge

of my foot. An orb weaver suspended between
the window and the screen, and twin

garden-variety spiders, frozen fireworks one inch
from the kitchen sponge, draped between the orange

and the salt. A soldier beetle guards the door,
shining elytra closed over

the wings neatly as the cover over piano
keys, as the gold leaf canopy

opens: the gypsy moth king wrapped in ermine
throbs the screen as if to say: *Behold this inhuman*

beauty: are you jealous? Yes, I am.
What a feat, to lay one's head down

on the ground zero of consciousness, where
armor unfurls its chrysanthemum petals right

from the bones, where the mouth is a scissors, and claws
creep under the shadow of wings

with venation more splendid than any rose
window—and then one surrenders

even one's ruthlessness, one's exoskeletal,
perfect self-control,

as these three cicada carapaces
kneeling on the screen. Some cool air

drifts through the window; one
cloud suspends the evening. I'm reading when

a mosquito comes singing to the valley
of my ankle. I raise the book to kill it,

but miss, and the mosquito wobbles for
the ceiling, a bubble in a pool,

then vanishes. Yet I hear it droning,
lecturing about what to attend to,

what to forge, what to lose. I ignore it,
crouching down again to read, inert

and resilient tonight as platinum.
Outside a car passes, glides its headlight down my arm.

Walking in the Dark

A tunnel of oaks and bats:
a hundred feet from my mother's house
and its three yellow fingerprints

of light, the dark bears down, its billows
recasting my skull. Then the meadow, open sky—
yet starless, and I'm folded

and plucked away. My mother can't remember
who I am. It won't matter if I'm gone
thirty minutes or thirty years.

She pretends it doesn't bother her,
as if what's merely personal
doesn't matter

on a fraying scrap of land each autumn blast
renews to original purity, a lithic
compression of fact

and loss. This:
Rhode Island, tucked under the arm
of Massachusetts, coaxed

by the ghost of a glacier, the firm-
ament loosening:
limestone ellipses laced with eel grass,

panic grass, yearly less
tangible. A low cloud crackles
the electric wire. Frogs creak

in the cattails and sedge,
electric; only in spring can one see
the frogs: pressed flat on the pavement,

translucent as paper lanterns. The lane
threads two brackish ponds which open twice
each year to the ocean's

egress, permitting
the boundless but in measured intervals.
Some animal ruffles

the margin, and a mile
further, the waves swell, the waves a rickrack
to bind each wrinkled

inch of the shore, the waves
a serrated blade to fray the shore. A single streetlamp
spoons a limpid

wedge of moths from the dark
and throbs its halo into my head,
blinding me:

but I know: a hundred feet
and a snag of beach plums and rugosa roses, a reel
of cord grass pours

for the edge. I keep walking.
My body drifts apart, weightless,
my head full of rushes

and shale, my own two brackish ponds in their orbital
escarpment, bitter,
opening. Tonight, no moon,

and each wave a gray thumb rubbing and rubbing
as if to erase each recognizable gleam.
Sometimes it must be a blessing

for past and future to chip away, leaving one merely
with sense—and here's my rock. By day a rise
of red granitic gneiss

the size of a sleeping cow,
tonight it joins obscurity's chorus: retreating blue-black
amid the plucked-

away planes of water and earth.
This: my rock, my ark, my raveling
foothold; the waves envelop

and cast it away,
repeatedly. I always perch here to scan
the ocean (or now, just to listen).

Tonight the tide's high,
and a plover still calls—day too cluttered
with the sonic glitter

of visible birds—its *keep-*
keep always solo
and ringing the dark like a chisel.

View from a Temporary Window

Follow the wrecking ball: in a month, it will smash
into this glass

like that housefly. A blueprint unfolds on a table
beside an orchid doubled-

over with white blooms, and out the window, just half a bridge
dives into the front page

of a newspaper the neighbor lifts from her balcony.
Partial to more, we're beckoned

outward, beyond the foundation: a new picture
window will jut

over the cliff to frame all the Golden Gate's
red seismograph, which cuts

through the fog to the headlands. In a year, in wing-back chairs
we'll sit in the air

high above those tiny people strolling
the crumbling sill

down on Bay Street, out there where the orchid's reflection
hovers with a flock of gulls.

ERIC MCHENRY

Eric McHenry was born in Topeka, Kansas, in 1972. His first book of poems, *Potscrubber Lullabies* (Waywiser, 2006), won the Kate Tufts Discovery Award. He lives with his wife and two children in Topeka and teaches at Washburn University.

Rebuilding Year

After Beloit I went back to the paper
and wrote arts features for eight dollars an hour,
and lived in the Gem Building, on the block between
Topeka High with its Gothic tower
and the disheveled Statehouse with its green
dome of oxidizing copper.

I was sorry that I had no view
of old First National. Something obscured it
from my inset balcony. I heard it
imploding, though, like Kansas Avenue
clearing its throat, and saw the gaudy brown
dust-edifice that went up when it came down.

Friday nights I walked to High's home games
and sat high in the bleachers,
and tried to look like a self-knowing new
student, and tried not to see my teachers,
and picked out players with familiar names
and told them what to do.

Fire Diary

Setup: what
do you get
when you cross
the road? Wait.
I placed my loss.

Setup: what's
so funny about

preserving the halitat's
natural habibut?

Nancy? Answer:
"Sir, you're drunkfish."
—Nancy Astor
Nancy, what's burning?
Nancy, you passed
out without turning
off the monkfish.
Nancy, the stove.
Nancy, you're an
alcoholic.

Nancy, this morning
the alc and hallcove
smelled like last
night's disaster
and minced garlic.
Nancy, that's
a nasty habibut.

Nasty, you can
have that bluefin
one of two ways:
Setup: why's
Nancy's place
like a halibut?
Punchline: gutted.

Setup: what's
the difference?
I lost my place.
Punchline: flooded.

* * *

Vulgar, like champagne
from a slipper,
there's been rain
on piles of paper.

The pimpled ceiling
looks like a river
that, while boiling,
has frozen over.

The books look fine,
but most were either
exposed at the spine
or flush with the wall,

and falling water
can only ride
a wall until
it meets a ledge,

so it will turn—whether
my books are dry—
on what I judge
my books by.

I look. Inside
each one, the dark,
stale, inscrutable
watermark.

Point Lobos

was something, but in pictures it's another
planet, with its three-inch facsimile
of cousin, second cousin and stepmother.
A handsome, figurine-scale family

clambers over the stone-studded faces
of newer stone, eccentric tidal scape,
sandmasonry, sand sanded into mesas,
committed by the kilning to its shape.

That day is in no danger. The sea otter,
belly-up in the bed of kelp, won't wake
to find a riptide taking him. The water
can't come for us. Those waves will never break.

Grandparents paid for everything. The sun
sent salutary beams from outer space,
and burned us, we would learn, but in this one
it only dulls the hard lines of my face.

No Daughter

No son. Son.
One life is mine;
my days can barely contain
themselves. I sleep in
the eggshell of zero.
My body says one.
The clock says one. I go
to the sink for water.

Son, no son.
Daughter, no
daughter.

A father has a son,
or daughter,
one born soon.
A son born early.

It's still early.
He has seen him through
the glass, seen
him clearly—
length of a pen,
radishy skin,
the clock says one,
the respirator.

In his sleep, when
he sleeps, he dreams
a daughter,
maybe a twin.
And he breathes at her.
One, two,
three, four, five,
she is alive, breathing in
the incubator.

Breath like water
drawn, drawn.
No son, son.
Daughter no daughter.

Figurative North Topeka

For Ben Lerner

Seasonal graffiti crawls
up the overpass like ivy—
abstract names on concrete stanchions.
To the south, symbolic walls:
NO OUTLET signs along the levee,
idle river, idle tracks,
bypass, bluffside and the backs
of Potwin's late-Victorian mansions,
flush like book spines on their shelf.
Drunk on your late-Victorian porch
you promised me that if elected
you'd have the river redirected
down Fourth Street, to make Potwin search
North Topeka for itself.

I told you to retire *Ad Astra*
Per Aspera and put *For God's*
Sake Take Cover on the state
seal and flag—the license plate
at least, since we collect disaster
and loss like they were classic rods:
'51 Flood; '66 Tornado.
Even the foot-lit Statehouse mural
has a sword-bearing Coronado,
a Beecher's Bible-bearing Brown
and a tornado bearing down
on its defenseless mock-pastoral,
The Past. The present was still wet
when the embarrassed legislature
resolved that it would never let

Eric McHenry

John Steuart Curry paint the future.
He never did, although Topekans
would learn to let bygones be icons.

* * *

On Thursday, July 12, the rain
relented and the water rose,
darkened and stank more. The stain
is just shy of the second story
in what used to be Fernstrom Shoes.
That entire inventory
spent five nights underwater, gaping
like mussels on the riverbed.
Fernstrom spent the summer scraping
gobs of septic-smelling mud
out of eleven thousand toes.

On Friday the 13th, the Kaw
crested at thirty-seven feet.
They thought it might have cut a new
channel down Kansas Avenue.
One *Capital* reporter saw
a kid reach up from his canoe
and slap the stoplight at Gordon Street.

Porubsky's never did reclaim
its lunchtime clientele; the torrents
sent the Sardou Bridge to Lawrence
and there was no more Oakland traffic.
Business hasn't been the same
for fifty years now. Fifty-two.
Ad astra per aspera: through

the general to the specific.
You do what you want to do
but I'm not using North Topeka
in conversation anymore
because there is no north to speak of;
there's only mud and metaphor.

"Please Please Me"

I don't love the Beatles. No one need
ever publish or anthologize
this poem now. To those who manage to read
this far into it, I apologize.

My girlfriend has said, not knowing she'd
end up in a fifth line, "Them's fightin' words."
I know. I know they gave me Alex Chilton,
who gave me the best of Big Star, through the Byrds.
I know their sound and am not ignorant of
their catalogue. I know it begins with "Love
Me Do" and takes a slow turn for the sallow,
maturing toward those white and mustard-yellow
albums everybody says are golden.

That's why I'm confident no one will see
this stanza. By now I've lost even readers
of poetry, who love their losing battles,
but not quite as much as they love the Beatles.

I believe in the many primacies of taste,
and in doing nothing to dislodge its nest

from a dependable cleft in the soul's one tree.
That's really why I don't love them: because
they make me feel like it's only me,
which is so unlike what so much music does.

The Swallow Anthology of New American Poets

MOLLY MCQUADE

Molly McQuade was born in 1961. Her poems included
here belong to a group on which she worked as the writer
in residence at the James Merrill House and, soon after, as
an artist in residence at the Art Institute of Chicago. Her
writing has received awards or fellowships from the New
York Foundation for the Arts, The Pew Charitable Trusts,
PEN, and the National Council of Teachers of English,
among others. Her books are *Barbarism* (Four Way Books,
2000); *Stealing Glimpses: Of Poetry, Poets, and Things In
Between* (Sarabande, 1999); *An Unsentimental Education:
Writers and Chicago* (University of Chicago Press, 1995);
and *By Herself: Women Reclaim Poetry* (Graywolf, 2000). She
has taught at the Poetry Society of America, Johns Hopkins
University, the Unterberg Poetry Center, Rutgers Univer-
sity, and the School of the Art Institute of Chicago. She lives
in New York City.

Artisan, Expired

Oh abolish this, they must have sighed—
those scriveners striving with their inlay,
an ether oddly cursive,
smittening a desk in some low chamber or cave.
Their bosses, the bureaucrats
of shah or sultan, poof a command their way
as the sun rises. The glass-blowers snap and flame.
And so the fineness of an artisan
is unloosed on a metal ewer, a bier.
He is engraving his Mesopotamian calm of day
on the coiled nest of accosting dragons
conniving in a brass niche,
and on his solitary iris, almost an insult,
pouting in a silver sway of candlestick—
the carvers and carriers follow a song to the skies
in drastic geometry.
They hope for ablution, annulment,
assuaging, the iris.
A river dwells with them, donor of
all star-tiles with twelve dripping lapis tails.
They have sculpted God's machinery,
installed interlocking stillnesses,
built a bone garden, the Elephant Water Clock,
medallion spun from medallion.
Made by Uman ibn al-Haji Jaldak,
the apprentice of Ahmad al-Dhaki al-Naqqash al-Marsiki . . .
His brazier, the bryony stem drawn on it, an acacia demanding,
the pious domes near the alcove, a lobed archway,
polygons embroidered staccato on the ceiling,
an adroit astrolabe

meant to measure the nothing in anything—
it is all a narrow pomp in an atelier.
They coveted a refuge, lived like cherished slaves,
walked a flotsam of nacre,
God's pupils—an ellipsis.

Lives of the Jewelers

Take cover
before the "rigid bangle,"
called *jonc* by Georges Fouquet:
Hungarian magnates
and Munich goldsmiths
would turn Nature into artifice,
"the mountain of hell
become like amethyst"
—and we'd be left to wonder.

"Her dog collar was not adjusted
to fit her neck closely," complained a husband
of that *collier de chien,*
"and the rows of pearls
droop slightly
in consequence."

And then,
"dog collars were often very wide";
the Duchess of Marlborough's "rasped her neck,"
while the wings rising behind
the Marchioness of Tweeddale's tiara
have been tickling her.
But So-and-So wouldn't

make repairs even
for La Bernhardt.

Among themselves,
gemologists hardly ever agree,
and besides, many are smugglers.
"Minute flakings on the girdle"
marred the Jacob diamond
of the sixth Nizam;
for a full year someone
in Amsterdam cut
and cut at it while
the Queen of Holland squinted.

Facets smart with *ichor*,
and a spurt will wound.
Even mining methods can endanger:
"Crowbars were used to dislodge the rocks
which were then further broken
up with hard blows"
in the diamantiferous Deccan.

Riches have been known
to go astray, as when
the elderly Osman ali Khan
"insisted on living on
less than 7s 6d a week
and said he could not
make ends meet.
He was knitting his own socks,
bargaining with stallholders
over the price of a soft drink,

rationing biscuits,
　　and smoking cheap local
　　　Char Minar cigarettes.
　　　　A steady companion
　　　　　was a pet white goat
　　　　　　chewing on a turnip."
　　　　　　　Not even the *jugni marvareed*
　　　　　　　　could make much difference
　　　　　　　　to a life like that.

Pity the jeweler:
　　Dates of birth and death unknown.
　　Born in Paris.
　　　Workshop at 12 Rue Legendre.
　　　　Early pieces attracted little attention.
　　　　　(He would say to them,
　　　　　　"I like to look at people
　　　　　　who are looking at
　　　　　　what I bedeck.")

1923: Settles in Southern France.
　　Main activities include
　　　collecting, dealing, and carving
　　　alabaster containers.
　　　　(This, then, is the fruit
　　　　　of blister pearls,
　　　　　of cabochon opals?)

When the starlet wouldn't wear his *louche*
　　black poppy ornament,
　　　Lalique cleared his throat:
　　　　"The jewelry industry in general
　　　　lags behind the new ideas

by the usual fifteen
to twenty years."

And when Sonia Keppel went
to the theater with her mother,
King Edward's favorite,
another lady, arriving late,
groped her way to her seat
in the dark, removed her hat,
and pinned it to the back
of the seat in front of her.
"A scream . . . rang out."

Sonia soon beheld "the terrifying spectacle
of Sir Hedworth Williamson impaled
like a gigantic butterfly
on the back of his seat.
The stem of the offending pin
was probably some
14 in. to 16 in. long
and made of Sheffield steel"
in Halifax.

Buddhists, Left Hanging

Two more or less modest Buddhist figurines
have been left hanging,
poised to glint, scriven,
and swim golden as oppressed script
in the museum,
lunging on the lam
from a folio of Arabic's

filmy flyaway wisdom,
gilt-clinched and ink-begotten,
like sister maniacs moistened
by a masochism
in their cool, slim heaven.
These *apsaras* were chosen
by a loose and cloudy spirit
who pulled a page from the volume,
squeezed their noosed accordion lungs from it,
and launched the wrung, free beings up
with covetous hands folded.

Synchronized Swimming

"It took thousands of hours to perfect this single element,"
the sculpted placement,
a slim, moony niche in a mussel shell

schmoozing the severe pointillist frenzy
of the female Aquacade, 1996, Atlanta. Esther Williams
in her dotage sheds a tear in the stands, aglimmer

at all the flashing American thighs
in a fast fish bouquet. The crowd
strokes its own marbleized fins, alert

to a miracle.
The American team is a submerged Versailles
like we'd never dreamed of.

Bach, cross-dressing courtesan, our crony,
agreed to lend his favors for an afternoon
of sleek rivalry among women. "The swimmers

can hear the music very well underwater,
even better than they can above,"
pants the announcer. Some cellos

twirl on the half-shell,
their bass line plinking like devout pebbles.
Mecca is a water machine,

serenity of flanked chlorine,
and the nine-foot depth they all toe is an
afterlife the girls are not permitted to test

(if their penitent feet touch bottom by chance,
it's a point or two off).
The whorl of concrete is their muse.

Esther began it long ago,
natty in her spirochete swimwear for the underwater camera
mounted by Billy Rose,

and she is ashamed, at first,
that the Canadians seem to be doing better.
(They are very pert; they wait

to cross the ramp like colorblind walrus.)
But brilliance is relative, mainly,
and the splashed figurines of Saskatchewan

and Manitoba are nothing
as compared with American dilemmas.
The constant slippery smiles of our women

make them look like vampyre-dentists
sucking on wet, green enemas; now they wriggle
around *Afternoon of a Faun* snippets.

Their "quick, precise pattern changes"
are an armory of Victorian gladness,
kicked at in comeuppance.

They have trained for this moment for five whole years,
mermaids never far apart; most of them
are swimming today for the last time competitively.

On average, their hearts beat 180 times a minute for the full five
required in their performance
before, like drunk hummingbirds,

they gain on the palace.
And just barely. When all rise, the hailed champions
can say nothing,

make meek adjustments with their eyes.
Doctored water swivels down their elegant jowls,
their nippy groins.

Esther says,
"I can't swim fast, I don't *want*
to swim fast,

I want to swim *pretty*."

Before

Deep-set in a brown cusp,
seeds cringe from the stalk
and cling to the outstretched flower head,
stashed grudgingly.

Hardened, massy,
details seize: a coat sleeve,
sock cuff, will receive
these little-if-anythings.

Starlings shatter upswept
in another clasp.
The rustle of growing old,
before being born.

Pulse Grass

Profuse grass
to loll in is
what I wish
for toad, egret,
tidal snail.

The reverie
coursing lush
of grass
about to be
a home

would keep
the claw that
crept, the beak
that cropped,
the tongue

that bore;
serpentinely
sweet, of course

the tufts
will meet

and part,
at rest
with clicking
selves
asleep.

Photo by Talia Neffson

Joshua Mehigan was born in 1969 and grew up in Johnstown, New York. His first book, *The Optimist* (Ohio University Press, 2004), was one of five finalists for a 2005 *Los Angeles Times* Book Prize and winner of the Hollis Summers Poetry Prize. He has lived in Brooklyn since 1992.

Promenade

Bowne Park, Queens. Labor Day Morning. A man stumbles
across a wedding.

This is the brief departure from the norm
that celebrates the norm. The wind is warm
and constant through the field set at the heart
of the impervious borough, yet apart.
This day and this place, born from other days
and places as a parenthetic phrase,
and this sky, where a businessman may write
the purposeless, brief beauty of a kite,
are like the possibilities of love.
The kite leaps up, rasps fifty feet above
until it is almost unusual,
and fastens there. The wind's predictable
but private method with it sets it free
to dive toward greater plausibility
and finish its digression in the wide
municipal burlesque of countryside.
What distantly appear to be festoons
of white, white bunting, trefoils of balloons
in white, improve the black affectless trees
where three girls stand like caryatides
patiently holding crepe bells to a bough.
Something exceptional will happen now.
But first, the fat, black, windswept frock will swerve
past the buffet to steal one more hors d'oeuvre.
He floats like an umbrella back to where
his book is, smoothes his robe, and smoothes his hair.
Yellow grass undulates beneath the breeze.

Couples file through the corridor of trees
toward rows of folding seats. Bridesmaids unhook
from groomsmen's arms. Every face turns to look;
and when the bride's tall orange bun's unpinned
by ordinary, inconvenient wind,
all, in the breath it takes a yard of hair
to blaze like lighted aerosol, would swear
there was no greater miracle in Queens.
Wish is the word that sounds like what wind means.

Two New Fish

Inside the knotted plastic bag he tossed
and caught in front of him the whole way home
were two new fish. They seemed to him to bear
a trademark not quite rare, as though the two
were penknife souvenirs from the next county.
The fish were alien and mediocre.

He felt his strength as if it were a bomb
that detonates with no complexity
of wires or clocks, fuse or even impact.
His tosses changed without much thought to heaves.
They arced, slowed, hung like miniature flames
trapped in a bubble, glanced the power lines . . .

The fish sped back an inch and forth an inch
in the bag cupped in the boy's hands, and then
not in his hands at all, then on the grass.
He rolled the bag experimentally
over the gravel drive to demonstrate
again how well he kept from breaking it.

He hung it on a stick and jabbed the air
fitfully, like a hobo shooing bees.
He did his undecided best to burst
and also not to burst the bag. And when
within these limits neither fish had died,
the boy put down the bag and went inside.

In the Home of My Sitter

Mrs. Duane Krauss, sure of her solitude,
grimaced between the kitchen alcove's cryptic
lesser motifs of Elvis and Saint Jude,
herself the central subject of the triptych:
her young-old country cheeks and looming bust,
the timely smile, gathered around a lie.
She called me "dear," she bowed, she briefly fussed,
then turned to pat her mother's china dry.

I did my part. I showed how bright I was,
how self-assured. But I lacked common sense.
Even the dogs there knew—and not because
she humbled them with cozy sentiments—
that friends, not being family, not quite,
keep out of trouble and keep out of sight.

*   *   *

Across the white hill swallows fanned and scattered,
drawing my eye along till I could see
atop the hill—tilted and mossy, flattered
by early sun—an old barn, tempting me.
Morning to suppertime not much else mattered.
They must've known. I wanted them to know.

Morning to suppertime their still den chattered
with *Meet the Press* and Christian radio.

Patient, I watched the barn's roof simplify
to silhouette, and the hillside's azure glow
pass, as the night retuned my errant eye,
to static white, the white of moonlit snow,
while those four faces I've not seen again
kept to the borrowed twilight of the den.

*   *   *

One face there, bright as ripening persimmon,
still a bit bitter, seldom looked at me:
that quiet *Vater* stooped amid his women,
who let his lenses flash for privacy.
High in the shadow of a naked rafter,
his stuffed barn owl outspread its furious wings,
a household daemon to discourage laughter,
unnecessary talk, and touching things.

*   *   *

Mother, my young, my beautiful rescuer!—
so late, so long, I might be waiting still,
my pure heart wondering always where you were,
if not for those four strangers on their hill,
who, loath to form a fair impression of me,
simply did not, as you must always, love me.

The Optimist

The film showed stars of varying magnitude,
the left side Libra, and the right side Cancer,

mapping the brain's horizons, vanishing points
respectively of reason and desire.
The doctors liked her cheerful attitude,
hope being all she had in her position.

She waited, calm. Touch burned out first, then vision.
Emotion slipped. Last would be lungs and heart.
But, noting trends, they told her taste was next.
She asked then, could they pick out her last dress?

She wasn't making light. It seemed to her
that cancer just rehearsed life's attitude
that one's desires must taper to a point,
which has position, but no magnitude.

Rabbit's Foot

Grandfather rabbit, and grandfather hare,
forgive us, your forgetful progeny,
who unleash dogs to shake you in their jaws,
then sell your hacked-off hands as souvenirs.
Forgive us. Our hearts, too, are very little,
and race with blood as tenuous as our fate:
We also tremble helplessly or flee.
But, with this relic of your ancient luck,
so may we also often procreate,
and burrow always toward the mystery
below, as our grandfather rabbit does.
And may our naked children, as yours do,
grandfather hare, drop always open-eyed
onto the sunlit meadow of despair.

Merrily

> "And we sleep all the way; from the womb to the grave we
> are never thoroughly awake; but passe on with such dreames,
> and imaginations as these . . ."
>
> John Donne, "Sermon XXVII"

If only their significance were clear.
This quick, green bank. The sun's autistic eye,
oblivious to one more pioneer.
Unmeaning blue, less sky than anti-sky.
West, through the trees' meshed crowns, light scattering
toward such specific ends! Why those? And why
these flexed roots? Why that oak's failed rendering
of coupled elephants in living wood?
Its leaves smell sour, although it feels like spring.
I could go on. *Quis homo?* It's no good:
The more things blur, the clearer I become.
I could go on forever if I could.
Meanwhile, my boat moves downstream, listing some.
The question tails away. Against the prow
pumped gently by the surge, my back goes numb.
Behind, a riot-swept feather or split bough
neither recedes nor gains. As if to steer,
I drop a hand in. Oh, well. Anyhow,
the scenery is mesmerizing here.

Father Birmingham

Do you remember Father Birmingham
telling about the Sacrificial Lamb,
his little voice gigantic in the nave?
His septum looked like skin inside a pepper.

He loved the tale of Damien the Leper.
He stressed good works and giving, and we gave.

Bottomless glasses that, removed, laid bare
a foggy, oddly vulnerable stare,
the red, lined neck that smelled of aftershave—
sure, I remember Father Birmingham.
He's an important part of who I am.
He taught me not to be but to behave.

To Church School

The girls and boys
that stammer by
at one o'clock
stretch half a block.
Clouds follow them;
also, the steeple.

The tallest and others
waiting to see
what the tallest will do
tie parkas of blue,
yellow, or red
around their waists.

Already lost,
one boy had tied
a parka of red
around his head.
That boy now lies   .
shoved on the grass.

Joshua Mehigan

Ms. Bell, who ably
shepherds them,
and Mrs. Stack,
in the way-back,
coldly and clearly
chide, not holler.

The smallest pause
with giant eyes.
The sidewalk glints
at the innocents
so like people
only smaller.

Citation

Their ruler is elected state by state,
and no one cuts his heart out as he drowses.
Their senior citizens still copulate.
Their convicts are allowed to change their blouses.

In this backyard there hangs a gutted deer,
and in that driver's seat there sits a wife.
They have their MMR and Retrovir.
They have their quarter-century more life.

Each commoner receives a welcome mat.
The maids have maids, and plumbers go to Paris.
They call their waiters "sir." The poor are fat.
They eat. They do not easily embarrass.

The Swallow Anthology of New American Poets

Confusing Weather

The sun came to in late December. Spring
seemed just the thing that flattered into bloom
the murdered shrubs along the splintered fence.
The awnings sagged with puddles. Roads were streams.
Wet leaves in sheets streaked everything with rust.
The man who raked his lawn transferred a toad
too small to be a toad back to the woodpile.
In the countryside, he thought he spied the trust
that perished from his day-to-day relations.

His head was like a shoebox of old pictures,
each showing in the background, by some fluke,
its own catastrophe: divorce, lost friends,
a son whose number he could not recall—
this weather, nothing but a second fall,
ending, if somewhat late, just how fall ends.
Each day that week he sat outside awhile
and watched his shadow stretch and disappear.
Then winter followed through its machinations,
crept up and snapped the green head off the year.

Photo by James R. Peters

Wilmer Mills was born in Baton Rouge, Louisiana, in
1969. His first book of poems, a chapbook, *Right as Rain*,
was published by Aralia Press in 1999. His first full-length
collection of poems, *Light for the Orphans*, was published by
Story Line Press in 2002. His poems have been published
in the *New Republic*, the *Hudson Review*, *Poetry*, the *New
Criterion*, *Shenandoah*, *Literary Imagination*, and others, and
have been anthologized in the Penguin/Longman anthology
of *Contemporary American Poetry* (2004). Most recently, he
taught poetry at the University of North Carolina at Chapel
Hill, where he was Kenan Visiting Writer, 2008/2009. He
lives in Sewanee, Tennessee.

Rest Stop, Alabama

Even here the rows of urinals
Are "automatic-sensor-operated."
There's a laser eye that watches me
Unzip my pants so when I zip them up
It does the flushing for me seven times.

Above my head the ceiling has a speaker
Dishing out the sticky sentiments
Of country music, giving me advice,
Clichés and platitudes, that tell how not
To live my life.
                    Out in the lobby again,
A road map on the wall says, "You Are Here!"
And I can press a button near the map
To catch the weather service bulletin:
"It's partly cloudy in Mobile tonight."

I wonder why it matters if the clouds
Are out at night, but I remember how
Sometimes I've seen the stars go blank in places
And been told that it was flocks of birds
Migrating in the dark too high to see.

There's melatonin in their pineal glands
Behind their beaks to let them find their way
By sensing minute changes in the light,
Unlike my kind whose senses have become
So insignificant that only words
And widgets thought in words can get us home.

It's been reported on the radio
That certain cars are being made today
With GPS devices in the dash

So drivers needn't worry with directions,
Reading road signs, having to stop and ask.

And if you watch the sky at night you'll see
The orbits of the satellites that catch
And send the signals of the world, what song
To sing for whom, which urinal to flush.

Back in my truck I hang my head out, looking
More at the constellations than the road
As if to follow my nose and navigate
From star to star, as the crow flies, like geese
And all the hordes of fowl that need no sign
To beat the shortest course from A to Z.

Berkeley Café

Plate glass. Table edge. A chair.
I strike a photo-realistic pose,
My own, "Interior With Coffee Cup."
It's like a still life painting that reflects
What I've been learning from customers:
It's all still life this side of the world, behind
The argon gas of double picture panes
That gather our reflections from within,
How we're arranged like mannequins and props,
And cast each one of us as negatives
That superimpose, collage on decoupage,
To make a living hologram against
A frantic motion of the world without.

The glass is camouflage, a hunter's blind,
Where sitting quietly with breathy music

Playing in the corner, we can hide
Behind the flinch and fly, the glance and glare,
Of window shine.
                              We think, "if we sit still
We won't be seen. We'll be . . . anonymous."
But outside there's a streetman on the curb.
His face is red and swollen from rosacea,
Alcohol, and anger. Arms are flailing.
Lips are moving. But our glass is thick.
You can't hear what he's yelling, so he looks
Just like a dummy whose ventriloquist
Is also mute, or choking on his words.
The puppet speaks for him in pantomime.

What does he want? He watches each of us
And throws his voice against our picture window.
Then he looks at me and I'm afraid
He'll read my mind and rummage out the place
Where art appreciation lectures lie
In dormancy from college. Then he'll learn
To judge a still life painting by how well
Its stationary props create a movement,
Not on canvas, but inside the eyes
Of those who see it.
                              I can feel his eyes.
He knows I'm hiding something, and he's good
At picking the lock of false security,
Disarming passers-by to get a dime.
I'd tell him no amount of change would help.

But then he's in. He's got my two-cents-worth
That can't impede his side from crashing down
Around my comfort and complacency

That would, by facile arguments, refuse
To let him criticize the world my side has drawn.

I look him squarely in the eyes and see,
Despite the rage around his face,
How there's a quiet stillness in his gaze.
It doesn't hinder me from entering
The shotgun tenement inside his mind
Where on an upper level there's a hall
That leads past doors of muffled televisions,
Babies crying, and the clink of dishes.
At the end I see a vacant room
That looks down on the alley yard below.
The room is empty, nothing on the walls.
A shutter bangs against the brick outside
And he's the figure standing in the window,
Silhouetted, turning around just then
To tell me something's off about this picture.

The Dowser's Ear

     Empty cattle trailers
     Rumbled dummy thunder
Down the road all day, and now tonight,
Heat lightning flashes more of the same fake rain.
It's just as well. I couldn't get to sleep,
And now it ricochets across the sky
With empty loads of light. We've had a month
Of drought that tightens dirt around my pond.
The local wells are dry. But I've retired,
Threw out my wand. I hate this time of year.

Roux can burn if flour
    Sticks in skillet butter.
I've been cooking up a storm myself,
My daddy's filé gumbo recipe.
He used to be a chef on oil rigs
Until the hurricane. I heard the waves
That killed him, and I hear them every year.
It's emptiness that fills me. That's my skill.
I hear the vacant rain before it falls.
It's like the murmur of a spiraled shell.

    Hurricane weather, stewing
    Deep for landfall, spewing
Rain-a-plenty in the Gulf and here
In Tennessee they always have a lack
Of something. Two men called today for wells.
I told them both to go to hell, and now
They think I'm sinful, not used to my skill.
They stand to lose so much, but don't we all.
I lost a lot in Hurricane Camille
And even now can't hear the end of it.

    More heat lightning flashes,
    Absent rain that passes
Over clouds, and I can make it out,
Each gurgling current under withered fields,
Down kitchen drains. The neighbors think I'm crazy,
Up all hours, but they'll never know
The screaming voice inside a breaker's rage
Or how it simmers in my ear. I hate
The sound of water. Give me one good chance
To make it silent. I'd be right as rain.

Rain

I

My father's father called this morning,
Asking me to help him plow new garden rows,
Turn under summer's weeds and saplings
Grown too thick for work by hand with hoes.
His mule died years ago, but he still saves
The plow, so we connect a single-tree
Behind his tractor, and I pull him slowly
Through the garden, turning on command, "Gee-
Haw," all afternoon until he waves
For me to stop and pull up old tomato staves.
Before we finish the sky turns cloudy.

II

Rain drives across his pasture.
I pull the tractor under his barn in time,
And we stand facing the storm together,
Hearing scattered drops on the tin roof chime
Into a deafening roar of falling rain.
He holds his hat and hurries for the house.
I watch him as he nears the door, his shirt
Gone speckle-wet to dark, and now the douse
Increases on the barn. But I remain,
Disconnect the plow, and watch the rain
Cascade like melted glass from eaves to dirt.

III

I close my eyes and listen to the tin
Reverberating like a high-tide beach
Beneath the sound of ocean coming in,
A sound that whitens in the mind to leach

Away all boundaries of thought.
I smell his saddles where they hang on rope
To keep packrats from chewing up their seats.
Sweet horse feed, hay, Bag Balm, and leather soap
Instill this barn with memories of when he taught
Me how to work the plows his father bought
To plant his lettuce, mustard greens, and beets.

IV

The handles of his plow are as smooth as bone.
I hold them for a moment. The rain streams
Loud on the tin, a soporific tone
That draws my childhood up like vivid dreams.
I remember someone telling me, when I
Was only five, my glass of water came
From my grandparents' own artesian well.
It fascinated me that pipes could tame
Ground water rising in the dirt all by
Itself the way trees siphon toward the sky.
They sealed it off when water pressure fell.

V

And I have heard that rain stays underground
For twenty years or more before
It filters upward from the earth, unbound
And formless on the skyline's shore.
But I cannot remember being told
When my grandfather's well was drilled
Or where the piping rose to bend elbows
Of water in the house, and now I'm filled
With questions. Rain when I was five years old
Could still be drinkable and cold.
Childhood gurgles up and overflows.

VI

My grandfather stands on the porch, waiting.
The garden rows we plowed resemble graves
Laid side by side beneath the rivulet-writing
Of illegible epitaphs the rain engraves.
And as I run to him, the roar of rain
On tin diminishes as when sleep falls
Around my ears to silence every sound.
When I come home and my grandfather calls
For help, I show my age and don't complain.
I am alive, awake, and young to pain
That wells in him like water in the ground.

Morning Song

In the kitchen, my mother hums so low
And clear her song and morning voice
Sound like a cello, bowed for tremolo.
Some parts of the house are still asleep, by choice.
It's Saturday and not much to be done.
There may be squirrel-hunting later in the day
Or leaves to rake in the afternoon sun.
But now the kitchen sounds of pots and trays.
My mother's song fades in and out of what
She does. It's clear she stops to concentrate.
One spoon of baking powder, flour cut
With shortening, then song again. A plate
Of bacon interrupts, then she returns
To humming. The house becomes her instrument
And we, like sluggish bees, get up in turn,
Charmed out of sleep by her sung disenchantment.
Some mothers sing to babies in the womb;

The Swallow Anthology of New American Poets

Others give their children weekly lessons.
We were reared with music in the playroom,
At meals, and going to sleep. Comparisons
Like this are hard to prove but each of us
Has learned, by listening, to speak the tongue
Of instruments: my brother joined the chorus;
One sister learned the harp when she was young;
The other plays piano and guitar.
So here we listen for the household sounds
Of home: ice water pouring from a jar,
Forks, knives, the flour sifter's rhythmic rounds.
Each tone recalls our childhood's symphony
Of clanks and bangs that softened into notes
We later learned to read. The melody
Our mother hums this morning swells and floats
Across the room, and after breakfast, when
We go our different ways, she rests, then starts
Her kitchen-orchestrations all again
With movements we come home to learn by heart.

Wilmer Mills

JOE OSTERHAUS

Photo by Alison Paddock

Joe Osterhaus was born in Cleveland, Ohio, in 1960. His books of poetry are *Radiance* (Zoo, 2002) and *The Domed Road* (in *Take Three: AGNI New Poets Series: 1*, Graywolf, 1996). He was Tennessee Williams Fellow and Visiting Lecturer at the University of the South in 2005. He has also taught at Boston University, University College at Washington University, and the Krieger School of Arts and Sciences at Johns Hopkins. He lives and works in Northern Virginia.

The Aughts

Open a wind-buckled door
on 13′ or 1505;
touch up the lacquer on a crown
whose red flashed in reprieve

of displaced tenants, raking ash
bloomed from a backspun shell.
Some centuries rattle open, with
an off note, not a peal.

The first years may be trough years,
when guards in skeleton coats
heap sandbags, and a riverwall
veins, where a trash barge molts;

when drought papers the countryside
and aphids catch like frost
in crops, that, dying, spread pointillist leaves
in fields of interest.

A future, dense with spires,
may diamond the spray flung
in half-coves, near containment walls
that trap heat off a sun;

or blister with the spent fuel rods
that, dropped in echoing mines,
tick down, as the millennia
leaf quartz on chill red vines.

Now cameras pin door and street,
rubbing their grays to drives

where our days tore like cigarette foils
in '03, '04, '05

when carriers packed with body bags
left small tracks on the seas;
lights barbwired the capitals;
and bombers cracked the skies.

Food Lion, Winchester, Tennessee

From here, the line seems not to move at all;
back beneath a clock that diamonds the hours
with blushing vents of coke. At last, we crawl
forward, just as Tess, the salesclerk, lowers
her chin and yanks her cash drawer from the register;
            then taps out the short stacks
        of rust-green twenty-dollar bills.
            Her sub attacks
the bottles of a woman who won't look at her;
who tilts and prods a pin pad with a stylus.

Night sways at the lit boundary of the lot.
Downroad, a Lotto billboard dances with flies,
whose reels card strands of glare, and epaulet
a gambler shaking the bias from two dice
and a drum sunk in the embankment, gouged with rust.
            Inside, the clockwork mists
        track Raleigh's world: from a field
            of broad leaves, twists
of cured tobacco; and, from harbors gigged with rest,
a waxwork queen wept on a waxwork shield.

Once past a bivouac of pans and tents
the new arrivals check their pace, outmatched.
Wheels corkscrewing, they stop for condiments
and, by their ribbons, show the troops dispatched
to stations in the crescent gulf are family
      to some; acquaintances
        to many more. And those absences,
          drawn out so long,
weigh in their words and eyes. Though I chose differently,
who'll say for all of us: we're not that strong?

Three-Card Monte

Despite the worlds it spins off every day;
      the million worlds that lash out from changed plans;

coins tossed in fountains; unread letters; play
      of numbers in a bookie's notebook; chance

always casts its influence in a bronze
      manysided as a dealer palming a queen;

the Spanish Armada, broken by high winds,
      granting the fireships their pretty screen.

With lantern-jawed Nevada, chance affirms
      our difficulty with accepting just

one life, that, through an actuary's terms,
      inscribes a book-lined apartment with the dust

of a great reckoning: nothing will change.
      Or, in Vegas, everything, if we allow

flash pyramids their shrill uses of the orange
      corrosions heaped at day's end on a scow.

So too the tanned, white-haired receptionist
      who, sitting beneath a trademark, counseling many,

      sighed as she haloed a quick pick with a penny:
"If I get this, you won't see me for dust."

Next

The moon, a flint struck off the Capitol's
lit dome, weighs daybreak at a border fence
whose gaps, to those still waiting, seethe like shoals.
Fresh off the Hill, new heads of state announce
successes, to the click of the capped heels
on the boots of the guard at the tomb of the unknowns,
who processes, turns, and tucks his rifle butt
hard against his shoulder, as his free hand cuts

a nerveless arc. At dawn, the host dictates
a memo to the southern hemisphere
about the orbital decay of a tin star,
that, skipped white off the atmosphere, dilates
the guards' attention at a checkpoint, bright
with floodlight where a family sinks to its knees.
A ruined base camp mines his emphases.
Done, he walks a garden walled with light.

Joints frost in lockers near the docks, where cranes,
pivoting, swing containers down from ships
that change their provenance with each new sky.
In the far ports, gulls drop from riggings dense
as tariff stamps, then glide past fouled hulls
as guards stamp in the warehouse doors. Come night,
forgotten culverts sweat where hostages
tremble in cut light as the stepped-up guards

play flashlights over the razor-wired vents.
In the green zone, a statue, brusque as chain,
calls down a wind on gumwrappers and wire.
Its grimace at the host of cinderblocks
recalls the corpses, blindfolded in pits, whose night
bristles the rooftop antennas with rage.
Which bucks our F-14s, as their instruments
whirl toward a lit deck, burst hard through a black wave.

Song

Now of an age when time is everything,
we wake in the first light to slate gray birds.
     Sweeping in view
off shrouded trees, they peck and choke down curds
of suet; scold the menacing shadow; sing.

Honeycombed with song, our summer drags
ivy like barbed wire through the watershed,
     where, in stained pews,
saprophytic fungi ridge and spread
wrinkled ears to the snap of plastic bags.

Next spring, we'll sleep with the window open
listening to the blackbird's voluble plea;
    and when our love comes due
we'll hear within our words the window tree:
dragged by the weight of the moon, thick-leaved, misshapen.

Rainswept

For Gerald Mast

The cone of dirty light fixed on the wall,
the gears and shutters of the stalled projector
would busy him, until the sought-for frame
leapt out in grained, unnatural relief;
Buster Keaton, say, swan-diving toward a wave
that turns to a sand drift as he's still aloft
and then again to snow, in which his strokes,
timed to meet the long-since vanished tide,
betray, despite his puzzled deadpan, the strength
and coiled athleticism of a gymnast.
The trigger in his hand, our teacher would
advance, lit frame by frame, through the whole scene,
explaining in a sometimes hectoring tone
the composition of the frames, and treating

our comments as ill thought, too forward, or naive.
Yet, within that darkened room, the banked wind
polishing the guttered ice outside
to the stark white within a negative,
the narrative impossibility
of that small screen and whirring projector
reclaimed for me the hours that I'd spent
cocooned in movie theaters when young,

suggesting that I needn't be ashamed
of the many backlit scenes that filled my mind,
such as that moonlit terrace, where a pair
murmured intimately and watched a bonfire moon
wink in a glutted pool, until they climbed
a stairway toward a room whose shadows seemed alive.

One weekday afternoon in the tiled hall,
the thick door of the screening room shut tight,
the tinny sound of the piano, played
with a tenacious virtuosity
one could only think was his, filled the air;
the piece a thirties show tune, Gershwin or Moss Hart,
and his voice, a vibrant, borrowed tenor,
belting out the lyric with aplomb.
Finished, he opened the door, still humming,
and, with a humble braggadocio
made sweet by its transparency, turned round;
his wish to be praised, and his distrust of the same,
crossing in the glimpse I had of him.
What happened to his knowledge, which combined

the genres of the thirties, Althusser,
and Aristotle's notes on comedy;
was it occluded by the pain and sweat;
the rank taste of his final afternoons?
In Hollywood, the final scene would show
a slight man, shouldering a heavy sack,
who, stepping round a corner in the rain,
whistles a tune the orchestra soon plays
as the camera draws back to show the street's
white houses, deep trees, and overflowing drains;
but, be that as it may, we cannot hear

his footsteps as he stamps upon the porch
nor see the nothing that surrounds the set—
the coils of rope, the tinseled lights, the depths—

wherever he's arrived, accomplished and too young.

The Running of the Blues

Bronzed, haphazard sunbeams; a sky, cut through
by eye-flaws runneling from banks of cloud
toward the weak flints that trailed the receding waves;
we walked out far enough to watch the dunes'

inked hollows spread, and join, as evening
sprinkled opacity on the variegated water
like rust on the damaged grillwork of a car—
some fishermen ran past in twos and threes

and, dropping gear and tackle in the sand,
gazed into the sheared walls of the surf—
like a tray of spools bouncing down a stair
alewives were leaping from the breaking waves

and, straining forward, we too saw the streaks
of bluefish crowding toward the shore, to cut
the small fry off with the scimitar of air,
which grew electric with their dying: gulls

screaming as they wheeled down to pick off the few
leapt clear of the burst whitecaps and mist.
The fishermen in turn made short deft casts
and played out sagging lengths of line, until

the surging water snapped them taut; its weight
dragging at the checked reels, that ratcheted
and trilled in high short bursts. As one threw back
a too-small fish, you stepped closer, the wind

pressing your body through your rumpled dress,
and I felt your trembling as your still damp skin,
freckled with sand, flushed rough, smooth, warm; then slid
the moon from its wet pocket in the clouds.

As soon as their attack grew regular,
it stopped, and we turned back toward the pier, heavier
yet buoyed by the needling atmosphere;
the blue veins showing in our necks and wrists.

The shoreline neon staggering to life,
we slowed and watched a trident hook a blue,
the fish grinning and doffing a porkpie hat
as the tines withdrew; then walked on toward the pier

which ended with a burst view of the sky
but found the entrance boarded for the night.
Halting in the beautiful debris—
tiered cans in seaweed, polyps and glinting shells—

we chose a bar and sat down to a meal
pressed by the night drive still in front of us,
and argued pointlessly, and paid the bill,
and grew more awkward and too serious.

It was our shades who walked back to the car
and drove to Cambridge through the rising dew;
another shade who stayed to close the bar;
and, yes, a shade who says this now for you.

Joe Osterhaus

Photo by Phyllis Freels

J. Allyn Rosser was born in Bethlehem, Pennsylvania, in
1957. Her third collection of poems, *Foiled Again*, won the
2007 New Criterion Poetry Prize and was published by Ivan
R. Dee. Her previous books are *Misery Prefigured* (Southern
Illinois University Press, 2001) and *Bright Moves* (North-
eastern University Press, 1990). She has received numerous
other awards for her work, among them the Morse Poetry
Prize, the Peter I. B. Lavan Award for Younger Poets from
the Academy of American Poets, the Wood and Frederick
Bock prizes from *Poetry*, and fellowships from the National
Endowment for the Arts and the Ohio Arts Council. Rosser
teaches at Ohio University.

Street Boy

The afternoon slows down, the town in steady rain.
That one with the trendy chicken-plucked look—
hair a tufted circle on top, the rest shaved all around—
I can't really care about. Of course I hope
he grows up without totalling himself and his car,
but he's the clown in this act. He seems even
to know his place as unworthy twerpy follower
of the one no one would look away from for long,
whose James Dean stance, hands deep in pockets
of a rattily natty maroon corduroy blazer,
shoves his shoulders nearly to his ears.
Beneath the blazer, long sulked-in jeans,
oversized black boots. He lifts one
to kick a milkshake someone couldn't finish
standing on the sidewalk, and it lands on
its side, explodes and rolls a vanilla graffito,
expletive unfurling. Expressionless himself.
The other boy smirks before the rain douses
and sweeps it stupidly into the gutter.

Even if I were not invisible through this darkish window,
they would know how to erase me. Well, he would.
I would enjoy that, just to see how he would do it,
what sort of panache he'd pack in his shrug.
Raining harder, and the tuft-headed one shifts
unhappily under the Revco awning, pivoting
his whole body now and then to see what the one
I'm half in love with's doing, fifteen, maybe sixteen:
he's twitching in sublime irritation, lighting up
again, hard to do with both hands in your pockets
but he pretty much manages no problem, and now

comes the move that gets me. He strides out
from under the awning, a spotted Lucky sticking straight
from his lip, walks two buildings down and turns
at the corner so his back's to Main Street and me,
stands, his twitch becalmed at last, stands
without heeding his friend's pleading
jeering calls, you idiot, you idiot, you idiot,
stands hunched, not looking up or down,
and I can tell this is his moment, this is where
he'll break off, he's going to unload everyone,
he doesn't blink as he hawks up their nothingness
and spits, feeling himself filling with what's left:
he takes possession of his spirited bad luck for good
and mounts and rides it without moving a muscle, stands
letting the rain collect behind his collar and drench
his gloriously inappropriately maroon corduroy
and his hair that looks not combable by anyone
alive, wild and bunched even when the rain
has patted keeps patting at it harder and harder
like an obsolete humiliated hand that wants to
feed and fend for and in general do for him,
and he has turned his back at last on the clown,
and on Main Street full of clowns you can both see
and not see, who wouldn't dare try to keep an eye on him
or try to follow him from now on.

Internal Revenue

I have distracted rodents from their cheese,
Lured seasoned sirens with my melodies,
And brought some handsome statues to their knees.
        I could not beguile you.

Having faced your shoulder, back and heel,
Borne the treadmarks of your fortune's wheel,
Felt your indifference to what I feel,
    My heart would not revile you.

I've shelved all my abiding passion, stashed
My childish cares and organized my past:
Real property, junk bonds, trusts amassed.
    —I don't know where to file you.

Asceticism for Dummies

When it nests in your core, catches
Your inner eye, gooses your heart,
Gleams like a redeeming thing,
Don't love it.

When it feels like heaven in your hands,
Bathes your mind with the scent
Of a still undiscovered wildflower,
Forget it.

When it kisses you, turn away.
When it asks for you, don't answer.
When it croons, moans, whimpers,
Don't admit it.

Should it curve along your hips
The way your hips have always hoped,
Should it fit nicely into your rib cage,
Cut it out.

If it has borne you, dismount.
If it accommodates, move out.
If it comes to bless you (no-brainer)—
Damn it.

But when it blazes up in a field
You're speeding by too fast to see clearly,
To stop at or ever find again, go ahead:
Want that.

Letter to a Young Squirrel

It's never about how many nuts,
though I'm not one to say it hurts
to have a trunkful, and a few
stashed underground. Maybe too
some seeds, a thistle. Diversify.
You know the others would sooner die
than praise a single thing you've got.
They'd let it go to rack and rot
before admitting you'd done well.
Let them go to hell.
It can't be a question of resenting
station, since we're all tenanting
the same scrawny, pest-infested
neck of woods, scrimping nests
from nothing, strips of scratch
that stink when wet and must be patched
each year. Each year we're overcome
with all the piling up. Numb
from fatigue, but still the chatter
starts in. Gibes, digs. Nothing sadder.
What eats at them could eat at you.
What can you do?

Avoid the highest perch. And *run*.
Always bolt across the lawn.
Never look over your shoulder.
Get busy, stay busy. Act bolder
than you are, and keep your claws clean.
Don't be too friendly. Don't be mean.
You can't win! This sounds harsh,
but what are we? Tussocks in the marsh
of time. A skittish question mark
in low profile. (Avoid the park.)
Just look at that oak-fed fool
chuffing his beady mug at you,
like a mad setter with a cough.
You're new: he wants to scare you off.
Why can't they all just climb together
in peace? *Why* must one be better?
Why won't Chuck say where he finds
the pink soft filmy stuff that lines
his nest? You didn't see? It glows
in the dark! Bastard just goes
rigid, fixes me now with one,
now the other eye. Both half gone.
You're young: don't think too highly of
your nuts. Don't puff your cheeks with love;
you'll wear them out. Remember this:
Invest in work. All else is risk.
Go on, get cracking. Just watch me.
And stay away from my tree.

Subway Seethe

What could have been the big to-do
that caused him to push me aside
on that platform? Was a woman who knew

there must be some good even inside
an ass like him on board that train?
Charity? Frances? His last chance
in a ratty string of last chances? Jane?
Surely in all of us is some good.
Love thy bloody neighbor, buddy,
lest she shove *back*. Maybe I should.
It's probably just some cruddy
downtown interview leading to
a cheap-tie, careerist, dull
cul-de-sac he's speeding to.
Can he catch up with his soul?
Really, what was the big crisis?
Did he need to know before me
whether the lights searching the crowd's eyes
were those of our train, or maybe
the train of who he might have been,
the person his own-heart-numbing,
me-shoving anxiety about being
prevents him from ever becoming?
And how has his thoughtlessness defiled
who I was before he shoved me?
How might I be smiling now if he'd smiled,
hanging back, as though he might have loved me?

Aftermath

Smiled, *smiled* at loathsome Smits
but managed to avoid handshake
of guy who told hooker joke
to Therese, pretty good though,
sorry pal; remembered to thank Peggy
but reminded John of match
he lost, so sure he'd won that;

spilled wine on ivory carpet
but foresight to drink white;
left Therese in boring clutches
of Brad Hitchens, tax breaks;
but good restraint only shrugged
when she claimed I was "weaving,"
wasn't; left without kissing woman
with maroon lips slit skirt thigh
but pressed against on way out;
why the smile, Smits didn't first;
Helen a looker but that house,
jerrybuilt ostentatious & she
still squinty from lift, Therese could tell;
odd, own loathing tripled by own smile;
lost keys but found quickly
this time, ran light but remembered
to fill tank, Sunday night, back roads,
Smits still holding his promotion
over me, as if I cared,
and then to make a crack like that
thank god Therese not there
would never let live down;
still, the twit knows his Nasdaq;
made love maroon lips in mind;
will try to get market tip next time, but
no smile, not from me again he won't.

Before You Go

As one before moving to a strange coast
Is moved to plant perennials just
To be, briefly, in spring, remembered,
Still be part of land he can't stand
To think he'll never walk upon again;

As that one's child will press a shell
Into a chink of his closet wall
For the next child moving in to find—
His favorite shell, worn smooth by sand
With spirals that feel funny in your hand;

As a man who loves a woman
Who is leaving him for someone
Will leave a kind note in a book
She might not get around to reading,
Hoping she'll find it listlessly reading

So it strikes her—a spasm of time
Uncoiled—like lightning at the spine
(Though she might find it when she's old,
So much older it seems unreal,
But matters, what he felt and will still feel);

As one who softly sings in the church
Whose walls seem mutely to rehearse
The chants of others, centuries ago;
Who lights her votive taper of song
Feeling calm, unbodied, not alone;

As a mother who commutes will first
Plant silly notes and riddles in verse
Under toys in her son's room
And tucked in the pockets of his pants,
Hoping he won't find them all at once;

I leave these silent words with you,
To whom they may mean next to nothing now.

A. E. STALLINGS

A. E. Stallings was born in 1968. She studied Classics in Athens, Georgia, and now lives in Athens, Greece. She has published two collections of poetry, *Archaic Smile* (University of Evansville Press, 1999), which won the Richard Wilbur Award, and *Hapax* (Triquarterly Books/Northwestern University Press, 2006), which received the 2008 Poets' Prize, as well as the new Penguin Classics verse translation of Lucretius, *The Nature of Things*. She was awarded the 2008 Benjamin H. Danks award from the American Academy of Arts and Letters and has received a National Endowment for the Arts translation grant.

Asphodel

(After the words of Penny Turner, Nymphaion, Greece)

Our guide turned in her saddle, broke the spell:
"You ride now through a field of asphodel,
The flower native to the plains of hell.

Across just such a field the pale shade came
Of proud Achilles, who had preferred a name
And short life to a long life without fame,

And summoned by Odysseus he gave
This wisdom, 'Better by far to be a slave
Among the living, than great among the grave.'

I used to wonder, how did such a bloom
Become associated with the tomb?
Then one evening, walking through the gloom,

I noticed a strange fragrance. It was sweet,
Like honey—but with hints of rotting meat.
An army of them bristled at my feet."

Aftershocks

We are not in the same place after all.
The only evidence of the disaster,
Mapping out across the bedroom wall,
Tiny cracks still fissuring the plaster—
A new cartography for us to master,
In whose legend we read where we are bound:

Terra infirma, a stranger land, and vaster.
Or have we always stood on shaky ground?
The moment keeps on happening: a sound.
The floor beneath us swings, a pendulum
That clocks the heart, the heart so tightly wound,
We fall mute, as when two lovers come
To the brink of the apology, and halt,
Each standing on the wrong side of the fault.

Fragment

The glass does not break because it is glass,
Said the philosopher. The glass could stay
Unbroken forever, shoved back in a dark closet,
Slowly weeping itself, a colorless liquid.
The glass breaks because somebody drops it
From a height—a grip stunned open by bad news
Or laughter. A giddy sweep of grand gesture
Or fluttering nerves might knock it off the table—
Or perhaps wine emptied from it, into the blood,
Has numbed the fingers. It breaks because it falls
Into the arms of the earth—that grave attraction.
It breaks because it meets the floor's surface,
Which is solid and does not give. It breaks because
It is dropped, and falls hard, because it hits
Bottom, and because nobody catches it.

Watching the Vulture at the Road Kill

You know Death by his leisure—take
The time we saw the vulture make

His slow, hot-air-balloon descent
To a possum smashed beside the pavement.
We stopped the car to watch. Too close.
He bounced his moon-walk bounce and rose
With a shrug up to the kudzu sleeve
Of a pine, to wait for us to leave.
What else can afford to linger?
The eagle has his trigger-finger,
Quails and doves their shell-shocked nerves—
There is no peace but scavengers.

A Postcard from Greece

Hatched from sleep, as we slipped out of orbit
Round a clothespin curve new-watered with the rain,
I saw the sea, the sky, as bright as pain,
That outer space through which we were to plummet.
No guardrails hemmed the road, no way to stop it,
The only warning, here and there, a shrine:
Some tended still, some antique and forgotten,
Empty of oil, but all were consecrated
To those who lost their wild race with the road
And sliced the tedious sea once, like a knife.
Somehow we struck an olive tree instead.
Our car stopped on the cliff's brow. Suddenly safe,
We clung together, shade to pagan shade,
Surprised by sunlight, air, this afterlife.

Persephone Writes a Letter to Her Mother

First—hell is not so far underground—
My hair gets tangled in the roots of trees

& I can just make out the crunch of footsteps,
The pop of acorns falling, or the chime
Of a shovel squaring a fresh grave or turning
Up the tulip bulbs for separation.
Day & night, creatures with no legs
Or too many, journey to hell and back.
Alas, the burrowing animals have dim eyesight.
They are useless for news of the upper world.
They say the light is "loud" (their figures of speech
All come from sound; their hearing is acute).

The dead are just as dull as you would imagine.
They evolve like the burrowing animals—losing their sight.
They may roam abroad sometimes—but just at night—
They can only tell me if there was a moon.
Again and again, moth-like, they are duped
By any beckoning flame—lamps and candles.
They come back startled & singed, sucking their fingers,
Happy the dirt is cool and dense and blind.
They are silly & grateful and don't remember anything.
I have tried to tell them stories, but they cannot attend.
They pester you like children for the wrong details—
How long were his fingernails? Did she wear shoes?
How much did they eat for breakfast? What is snow?
And then they pay no attention to the answers.

My husband, bored with their babbling, neither listens nor speaks.
But here there is no fodder for small talk.
The weather is always the same. Nothing happens.
(Though at times I feel the trees, rocking in place
Like grief, clenching the dirt with tortuous toes.)
There is nothing to eat here but raw beets & turnips.
There is nothing to drink but mud-filtered rain.

Of course, no one goes hungry or toils, however many—
(The dead breed like the bulbs of daffodils—
Without sex or seed—all underground—
Yet no race has such increase. Worse than insects!)

I miss you and think about you often.
Please send flowers. I am forgetting them.
If I yank them down by the roots, they lose their petals
And smell of compost. Though I try to describe
Their color and fragrance, no one here believes me.
They think they are the same thing as mushrooms.
Yet no dog is so loyal as the dead,
Who have no wives or children and no lives,
No motives, secret or bare, to disobey.
Plus, my husband is a kind, kind master;
He asks nothing of us, nothing, nothing at all—
Thus fall changes to winter, winter to fall,
While we learn idleness, a difficult lesson.

He does not understand why I write letters.
He says that you will never get them. True—
Mulched-leaf paper sticks together, then rots;
No ink but blood, and it turns brown like the leaves.
He found my stash of letters, for I had hid it,
Thinking he'd be angry. But he never angers.
He took my hands in his hands, my shredded fingers
Which I have sliced for ink, thin paper cuts.
My effort is futile, he says, and doesn't forbid it.

Olives

Sometimes a craving comes for salt, not sweet,
For fruits that you can eat

Only if pickled in a vat of tears—
A rich and dark and indehiscent meat
Clinging tightly to the pit—on spears

Of toothpicks maybe, drowned beneath a tide
Of vodka and vermouth,
Rocking at the bottom of a wide,
Shallow, long-stemmed glass, and gentrified,
Or rustic, on a plate cracked like a tooth,

A miscellany of the humble hues
Eponymously drab—
Brown greens and purple browns, the blacks and blues
That chart the slow chromatics of a bruise—
Washed down with swigs of barrel wine that stab

The palate with pine-sharpness. They recall
The harvest and its toil,
The nets spread under silver trees that foil
The blue glass of the heavens in the fall—
Daylight packed in treasuries of oil,

Paradigmatic summers that decline
Like singular archaic nouns, the troops
Of hours in retreat. These fruits are mine—
Small bitter drupes
Full of the golden past and cured in brine.

On Visiting a Borrowed Country House in Arcadia

For John

To leave the city
Always takes a quarrel. Without warning,

Rancors that have gathered half the morning
Like things to pack, or a migraine, or a cloud,
Are suddenly allowed
To strike. They strike the same place twice.
We start by straining to be nice,
Then say something shitty.

Isn't it funny
How it's what *has* to happen
To make the unseen ivory gates swing open,
The rite we must perform so we can leave?
Always we must grieve
Our botched happiness: we goad
Each other till we pull to the hard shoulder of the road,
Yielding to tears inadequate as money.

But if instead
Of turning back, we drive into the day,
We forget the things we didn't say.
The silence fills with row on row
Of vines or olives trees. The radio
Hums to itself. We make our way between
Saronic blue and hills of glaucous green
And thread

Beyond the legend of the map
Through footnote towns along the coast
That boast
Ruins of no account—a column
More woebegone than solemn—
Men watching soccer at the two cafés,
And half-built lots where dingy sheep still graze.
Climbing into the lap

Of the mountains now, we wind
Around blind, centrifugal turns.
The sun's great warship sinks and burns.
And where the roads without a sign are crossed,
We (inevitably) get lost.
Yet to be lost here
Still feels like being somewhere,
And we find

When we arrive and park,
No one minds that we are late—
There is no one to wait—
Only a bed to make, a suitcase to unpack.
The earth has turned her back
On one yellow middling star
To consider lights more various and far.
The shaggy mountains hulk into the dark

Or loom
Like slow, titanic waves. The cries
Of owls dilate the shadows. Weird harmonics rise
From the valley's distant glow, where coal
Extracted from the lignite-mines must roll
On acres of conveyor-belts that sing
The Pythagorean music of a string.
A huge grey plume

Of smoke or steam
Towers like the ghost of a monstrous flame
Or giant tree among the trees. And it is all the same—
The power plant, the forest, and the night,
The manmade light.
We are engulfed in an immense

Ancient indifference
That does not sleep or dream.

Call it Nature if you will,
Though everything that is is natural—
The lignite-bearing earth, the factory,
A darkness taller than the sky—
This out-of-doors that wins us our release
And temporary peace—
Not because it is pristine or pretty,
But because it has no pity or self-pity.

The Catch

Something has come between us—
It will not sleep.
Every night it rises like a fish
Out of the deep.

It cries out with a human voice,
It aches to be fed.
Every night we heave it weeping
Into our bed,

With its heavy head lolled back,
Its limbs hanging down,
Like a mer-creature fetched up
From the weeds of the drowned.

Damp in the tidal dark, it whimpers,
Tossing the cover,
Separating husband from wife,
Lover from lover.

It settles in the interstice,
It spreads out its arms,
While its cool underwater face
Sharpens and warms:

This is the third thing that makes
Father and mother,
The fierce love of our fashioning
That will have no brother.

The Ghost Ship

She plies an inland sea. Dull
With rust, scarred by a jagged reef.
In Cyrillic, on her hull
Is lettered, *Grief.*

The dim stars do not signify;
No sonar with its eerie ping
Sounds the depths—she travels by
Dead reckoning.

At her heart is a stopped clock.
In her wake, the hours drag.
There is no port where she can dock,
She flies no flag,

Has no allegiance to a state,
No registry, no harbor berth,
Nowhere to discharge her freight
Upon the earth.

Photo by Lauren Bialek

Pimone Triplett was born in 1965. Her books include *The Price of Light* (Four Way Books, 2005), *Ruining the Picture* (TriQuarterly Books/Northwestern University Press, 1998), and an anthology of essays, *Poet's Work, Poet's Play* (coeditor, University of Michigan Press, 2008). She was the winner of the Larry Levis Poetry Prize in 2003. Currently an associate professor of creative writing at the University of Washington, she also teaches at the Warren Wilson MFA Program for Writers. She lives in Seattle.

To My Cousin in Bangkok, Age 16

What space is for, to the boy peddling
through smoke and traffic blast,
past curry stalls and lean-to yard
encampments, is to keep in place
the dreams of the dead. Each night
his mother, long gone, appears to him
with the same command, saying *get up,*
go out, take the ride now, so that mornings
he snakes across the city to the old house
that was once theirs. Out to tend what little
remains from her life among the living,
he comes crashing through last year's
pile of peach and lychee cans, wrappers
bleared by heat below the carport, and goes
inside to dust the table's one blue bowl.
He shoves his fingers down into the fuchsia
broken open beside the windowsill, moves
the TV from porch to den and back again,
trying to remember what she wanted.
It takes all day to work these increments
of an intimate geography he'd like,
just once, to get right. Because there is always

behind him, you see, the one time he didn't.
Night his mother lay dying, he beside the bed,
there's the moment when she stopped
shaking and he made his first mistake,
thinking *now she'll be all right.* As she went
cold he covered her body with more blankets,
so she could sleep, and after that he left.

How the room must have darkened then,
small bed filling with that new weight.
And now if he comes back, fills the bowl
on her table with clear water, gauging
its cold for a second in this house
where he was born, the one she gave him,
it's to test his bit of the absolute, plunging
his hands, almost a man's, into the blue.

Spleen

Let's hear it for spleen, for how it survives
nine times ninety-seven lives, rutting in
all that's stubborn—the gene pool, elephant's
ass, dirt's secret deal with a fossil,
the fat boy whose bat it is. Spleen, ever
moving, nursed on the tits of a troll under
a bridge, reared in heat smashed to infinite
paw prints, the cougar pacing its cage. Here's
to the full stadium, the beer jockey
selling spleen, making his way down the rows,
remembering his deadbeat dad. There's
a girl in the ladies', third stall from right,
spelling out spleen with her own blood, tracing
the graffiti couplings of others. And as

for my spleen I say it's pure of heart.
I've let it grow all alone, a potted
plant in the dark, eating dust, old dish suds,
coffee grinds, cracked-at-the-half eggshells.
With river's mud I've tucked each and every

leaf into my body's first idea. What
else could pump me this wild with fury
and focus, this morning's vision of the one
who tried to steal my car keys, honor, candle, soul.
My enemy's been sighted, he's huffing
and puffing, he's riding a pricey tricycle
through traffic. Spleen says what's mine is yours
and his. Together we drive all night, break
into his house to shave all our secret
spots with his new razors so he'll never
know why his day is that much
duller. Memory's long for me and my spleen.
So give us back whole histories boxed
in the basement, jars of pennies, glass eyes,
plastic pearls, all the kid's leftover life-glut,
we can't waste a thing. Once I heard someone
say a body doesn't need a spleen. O
sanguine us not, dear rage, blessed bile, but
keep us long in the pain put there to make
us move—dear Spleen, keep us steady,
keel us past the reasons.

Bird of Paradise Aubade with Bangkok
Etching Over the Bed

Woke to hear you refuse
to stop working in heavy rain, shoveling the mud
that beggars our part
of the yard. After a while, I heard the rasp of iron's
rake on gravel, wet earth, your bending for the gaps
to get the seedlings right. Then for hours from the window

I watched all your muscles connecting up, your body's parse
of sweat and salt, hollows
between the ribs appearing, then not, around your
            breath's steady reed and thrum. Watched,
you see, until I knew, for once, I wouldn't try to leave.
Though I did want to walk out and say something else

    about moving through the myth
of ask and answer once. I wanted to tell you how I saw it spill
out on sidewalk, alleyway, underpass, and how traveling
            that way, in another country,
I had to love the hawkers' come ons,
their peddling, every night, the Leda and swan-style

    tracings. On our wall now, I can make out her limbs
misted in chalk blear, the thighs streaked, but still skirting his will.
And when you come in I want to show you
            the half man, half bird, the one whose mouth
hangs open, his little razor-cut hungering of how much
he wants her. Or have you see how the span

    of white rivers between
them, the distance of missing they wed again
and again. The chalk drifts through
            the design. Outside, a real bird's rapid trill in flight
skirts the window frame. And now you're stepping over
the lawn's dropped

    branches, carrying the tallest stalks still hung with weeds.
Getting there, you say, giving me the ones almost in bloom.
After you turn away
            I put the buds to my mouth

to taste the skin before it breaks open, the bodies, newly green,
bound to root-pact, stem-line, moments before they fall.

First Child Miscarried

Out of blood bed
    and pelvic bone,
        out of the sex-shot ancient seas,

out of egg cell
    and slime maze, sperm
        trip and secret code,

you slipped from the spiral,
    saying *no*
        to the flushed luck

of lung sac, the script
    in chromosome,
        amniote slush starting up,

saying *no* to the song
    of labor and gestation,
        the hard taking form, *no*

to vein tick and flesh time,
    no to ancestors branching
        from the family trees:

a shoemaker in Minsk,
    a general's friend in Bangkok,
        no to broom pushers in paper mills,

to lid-fitters in canneries, saying *not-to-be*
        descended from the green-eyed girl raped
        by Cossacks, from the draft dodger

of Czars' armies, *no* to smithies in small villages,
        millions migrating for the sake of better
        rice pits, nomads passing over

the by now long sunken land bridge—
        O my blotch and second heart-
        beat—saying *no*

to evolution, the men come from apes come down from
        boars and frogs and lizards,
        rejecting the swill

of molecules, the cluster of microbes—
        Oh let there be no amino acids,
        let there be no first star,

saying *no*
        to the *whowhatwhenwherewhy*
        saying *no reason,*

when you died inside,
        my smudge and promise,
        not willing to wait,

and who can blame you,
        wanting your first and final moment,
        free.

The Rumor of Necessity

I.

(Pattani, Thailand and elsewhere)

Again in the hotel of the head
                waters, it's all about
        the bird's nest soup.

Step one for the ancient elixir:
                boil one bird's nest, some rich stock, dry
            sherry, add egg whites to get this age-old

cure for impotence, which also brings
                long life. These days
            fifty of the half-teacup sculptures,

glued with swift work
                and saliva,
            can fetch a couple of K

on the open market. You can go there to see them
                as I have, spot where the winged
            architects shoot back-and-forth

inside a brick skull built near the river's
                beginnings,
            spit-balling their one thought

of home. Watch boys and men by the dozens,
                for pennies a day,
            shinny up the walls,

hammer and chisel strapped to their
                              slender limbs.
                    Each species willing to do

what it takes. First the male then the female
                         flies back to the empty
               ledge. In hot water, the nests separate

into long chewy strands.
                              You can garnish with green onions
               and ham.

          2.

Meanwhile the head of state
                         stating there has to be
               a firm hand, until

down the road everyone wants to know
                    who the heroes are, who the villains are.
               And maybe you read the one about two boys arrested

from a village with no name. Or pictured the police rushing
                         in, the boys suspected of dealing,
               coming as they did from the triangle of dirt

that starts behind our hotel
                    where once upon a people
               poppies were the cure. There must be

a firm hand. The boys forced
                         into "detox," then shoved down into
               the ground still alive.

Later someone in charge starts to think
                    and we can parse that too,
            the winged

synapse flying back and forth
                    inside his skull to build
            the bright idea:

pouring onto their heads the hot coals
                    and ashes, the urine
            and boiling soup.

Next day my mother
                    closed the paper,
            drove us to a temple

where midday sun splits the gold
                    face of the god she believes in
            practically in half. Outside, sounds of brake

squeals out on Mass Ave,
                    kids below us counting *nung, song*
            sam, see, the same

words she once taught me. We bent down to lay our heads
                    against the green acrylic
            carpet's little circle round the shrine,

said our prayers for the one boy who survived.
                    After weeks in the hospital
            it's the feet that can't be mended,

the skin shorn so cleanly off. I'm not saying
                    in that building
            we were heard. Back in the homeland

the birds in motion, attracted by music,
                    attracted by light.
            If you stand still you can hear them

ready to migrate, centuries of laying in caves given
                    up on. And when twilight arrives through
            the phone book thicknesses

of open slits in the hotel walls, you get their
                    slice in air,
            scissor sharp wings at full

dart and glide, their coming and going,
                    if you can make it out,
            like pages shifted in wind, echo and shriek

over eons shaping their talent to eat
                    a single mosquito
            in flight. There's the long build-up,

there's the boy who didn't make it. I'm related
                    to the heroes, related to the villains.
            I want to give you the firm hand. I want to thrust it

out now for you to take, every hour, every harvest, with the hundred wide
                    blade-on-a-whetstone
            bird scream going up.

CATHERINE TUFARIELLO

Photo by Jeremy Telman

Catherine Tufariello was born in Ithaca, New York, in 1963
and grew up in Buffalo. Her first full-length collection of poems,
Keeping My Name (Texas Tech University Press), was a
finalist for the 2005 *Los Angeles Times* Book Prize in poetry
and the winner of the 2006 Poets' Prize, awarded annually
for the best book of poems published by an American during
the preceding year. She lives in Valparaiso, Indiana.

Vanishing Twin

The pulsar of her heart
Kept time awhile with one
That shone as if through fog—
A slightly fainter sun,

Though not by much: both burned
Obscurely, light-years off,
As, with a fascination
That was not yet love,

We watched their beacons mapped
Against black depths beyond.
Now conjured, now concealed
Under the sweeping wand

That fixed their magnitudes
And axes on a chart,
How similar they seemed—
Two worlds, inches apart,

Blinking in synchronous
Morse code. We didn't guess
One signal would dissolve
In static nothingness,

Eluding our cupped hands,
A phosphorescent spark
Or momentary wish
Returned to formless dark.

What will this nameless face
Blurred in her own, this other,

Seem to her? Will she dream it
Sister or shadow brother,

Rival or counterpart,
Half-heard, fugitive rhyme,
Child in a frozen wood
Lost on the way to time?

Bête Noire

It blocked her path in the first bad dream
She could make me understand—
Tall and shaggy, with three dog paws
And a little human hand,

Unseen until—here she looked at hers,
Describing in the air
A gesture of menace, or warning, or welcome.
Either it ended there,

Or else she didn't have the words
To say more, at not quite three.
It held out its hand, she said again.
It held out its hand to me.

I rocked her and sang, assuring her
With a mother's instinctive guile
That dreams weren't real and couldn't hurt her,
Knowing all the while

That when she slept, the *tick-tick-tick-*
Tock of its stumbling tread

Would shadow me familiarly
And lie down beside my bed—

Accosting me with its rheumy eyes,
Its smell of damp defeat,
Its matted fur aseethe with fleas,
Its breath like rotten meat,

Its pitiful, imperious
Howl like an infant's, and,
Most appallingly of all,
Its apprehending hand.

Jigsaw

Six months ago, it made her cry.
Furious, looking just at shape,
She tried to force a swatch of sky
Into the chestnut stallion's nape,

But now she sees the picture too.
She chooses, studies, turns a piece,
Cajoling out of broken blue
High mare's-tail clouds and wheeling geese,

And from this mottled brown infers
The muzzle of the piebald foal.
Intractable particulars
Allude to their imagined whole,

A world to which she palms the key.
Her guesses are no longer blind

But purposeful; her strategy,
Patience and insight intertwined.

The red-roofed farmhouse and the rows
Of corn are conjured, hills condense,
And inch by inch, the meadow sows
Itself beneath the weathered fence.

The final piece is placed and locks:
Between the black mare's hooves, a plume
Of purple flowers—asters? phlox?—
And sprays of scarlet paintbrush bloom.

The Escape Artist

I.M. Michael Donaghy, 1950–2004

"My people were magicians."
"The Excuse"

I dreamed last night that you were at the door,
A little pale but brimming with your joke,
And we were thunderstruck, but not surprised
At being taken. How could we not have known
You'd reappear at the pub some rainy evening
And buy a round, your death revealed unreal,
Merely the latest, though a masterstroke,
In the litany of fakes and forgeries,
Hoaxes and pseudonyms you'd reveled in?
Too late, we now remembered, feeling foolish,
The deadpan "Seven Poems from the Welsh"
You'd claimed, in your first book, to be translations
Of an obscure medieval poet, Sion,
Who wrote them on the eve of his beheading,

And which you had the pleasure of hearing praised
By gossiping literati at a party,
None of whom believed when you confessed
You'd made them up. And there was the bad review
You ghostwrote of your second book, deploring
Donaghy's tics, his immature refusal
To give up playing games and find his voice.
The joke of a ventriloquist: why settle
For just one self when you could conjure many?
Faking your death, we saw, was just like you,
A trick you even practiced once or twice.
Collapsing suddenly in some public place,
How nimbly you'd make light of it (and art),
Telling the shocked crowd that you'd been felled
By "a sort of gypsy wedding in my heart."

As always, you were a party we couldn't leave.
After a while it seemed you'd never gone,
Hoisting a Guinness and drawing off the foam,
Lifting your flute and launching ("Listen to this!")
Into another we'd never heard before,
And, as the windows grayed with breaking dawn,
Regaling us with how you got away:
The twisted chain, its lock intact, shrugged off
By a sort of straight-armed stepdance; then your chest
Divested of its hoarded breath; your arms,
Sheathed in their canvas sleeves, worked slowly up,
Straining, straining, till your fingers grazed
The straps in back that, yielding, would allow
The whole contraption to be wrested free—
With a flourish no one had been there to see,
Though we saw it now.

Mary Magdalene

The squabbling soldiers gone, the women got
What fell to them. Beneath the drooping eyes
Of Pilate's guard (the afternoon was hot)
They laid him out and shooed the stinging flies,

Rubbed linen strips with myrrh and aloes, rinsed
The dust from limbs whose wounds no longer bled.
As if the crown still pressed there, Mary winced
When, with a separate cloth, they wrapped his head;

And she recalled the pressure of his palm,
The scent of spikenard, Simon's baleful stare,
And how, the whole house filling with the balm,
She wiped his wet feet with her loosened hair.

Days later, at the empty tomb alone,
She thought first of his pierced and broken feet
And wept, incredulous. But he was gone,
The wrappings, neatly rolled, still faintly sweet.

A gardener was bending in the shade
Among the gravestones. Trembling with dismay,
She cried, "Where is he? Tell me where you've laid
His body. Who has taken him away?"

He didn't answer. When she called again,
The stranger stood and took a step or two.
Her fear became bewilderment. And then
He said her name, and suddenly she knew.

The Mirror

The day after you say you do not think
You want to be married to me anymore,
I meet my own dark gaze above the sink,
Surprised to find my image as before.
The mirror faithfully reflects my face,
My compact body, solid as a stone,
Familiar shapes your words did not erase,
A vacant house I do and do not own.
Yet I feel invisible, a fragile elf
Wandering rooms vivid with ghosts of you,
Unreal, spectral, even to myself,
Expecting strangers' eyes to run me through,
This stubborn flesh to meet dissolving air.
One day I'll wake, and no one will be there.

Ghost Children

Trying to offer comfort, friends remark
How lucky it is we never had a child.
I nod agreement, knowing in the dark
They'll wake me, wild, inconsolate. You smiled
Good-naturedly when we debated names
After the wedding, wondered whether your
Features or mine would make the stronger claims—
My hazel eyes? Your hair, a black so pure
It is tinged with blue? Back home in Hawaii, you said,
Hapa children are known for special beauty.
I hoped they'd have your cheekbones, and instead
Of my pale, your golden skin. Now I mourn the pretty

Darlings I carry but cannot have, the ghost
Children whose faces are mirrors of all we've lost.

S'i' fosse foco, arderei 'l mondo

If I were fire, I'd set the world aflame;
If I were wind, I'd blow it down;
If I were water, I'd make it drown;
If I were God, I'd sentence it to hell.
If I were Pope, my pleasure and my fame
Would come from scamming Christians well.
And if I were emperor, know what?
I'd find some necks to cut.

If I were death, I'd fly to my father's bed;
If I were life, I'd flee from him instead;
And to my mother I'd do the same.
If Cecco were, as it was and is, my name,
I'd take the women who are young and lovely
And leave for others the old and ugly.

From the Italian of Cecco Angiolieri

Photo by George MacNaughton

Deborah Warren was born in Boston, Massachusetts, in 1946. Her poetry collections are *The Size of Happiness* (Waywiser, 2003), runner-up for the 2000 T. S. Eliot Prize; *Zero Meridian*, which received the New Criterion Poetry Prize (Ivan R. Dee, 2004); and *Dream with Flowers and Bowl of Fruit*, which received the Richard Wilbur Award (University of Evansville Press, 2008). Her poems have appeared in the *Hudson Review*, the *New Yorker*, the *Paris Review*, and the *Yale Review*. She lives in Andover, Massachusetts.

Anna, Emma

Anna, Emma, I turn to you—as experts
on adultery, though you're only fiction—
for advice on conducting an affair.
How to meet him, to start with. Not a ballroom;
not these days. At the office? At a bar?
How to manage the black lace, the mascara,
all the tricks that are wasted on a husband.
And I'd like a lesson in how to lie,
how to hide what will only get more flagrant
every day with the brazenness of habit.
How to handle the twinges of remorse!
And what to do when the novelty goes stale—
how to keep the romance's pages turning
faster when I can see the story's end.

Closing

When they sold a farm, along with a deed and witness,
they used to bring a handful of dirt to the table
and thunk it down on a cloth to close the deal.
They didn't need that inch or two of earth
to certify that the land was arable;
and it didn't vouch for more than a single field—
one pile of humus. So, what was it worth?

Not much, but I'd prefer the dirt to *this:*
Signatures, mortgages, notaries, lawyers, liens,
the covenants on the property being sold—
what do they have to do with a piece of land?
Passing papers—nothing's here to hold.

The dirt would show what the transaction means.
An earnest of the farm it's taken from,
the purchaser could weigh it in his hand.
Not much; but then a little heap of loam
is an amount I ought to understand
with the odd affinity I feel for home.

                  Randolph, Vermont

Third Person

Sometimes I turn myself from flesh to fiction,
becoming a character seen (in my head)
from a story's point of view, by an omniscient
writer—from outside me, where I picture
I and me as she and her instead.

Mostly, living inside my own first-person
mind is the perspective I prefer;
it's hard enough to make my biased version
true to the protagonist, and—worse—
I might not find enough to like in her.

Flight

Explain again what lets a swallow fly.
I've heard it all—the principles of flight—
how shape and speed and simple flow of air
can keep a hawk or heron coasting there:
It's not enough. There must be something else
(beyond two dumb wings paddling at the sky)

that lifts the eagle into empty height;
something at work before the first bird flew—
before the silly clanking pterosaur,
before the worm and weed were there, before
the heavy world was hanging in the blue;
so tell me again what agency propels
the starlings through the sky—what other thing;
what trick of physics, what third hidden wing—
what force that doesn't let the sparrow fall,
without which there would be no bird at all.

Regret

Now, in the last few days before the maples
open their yellow-knuckled fists
and take the air in green hands—it's the day
they've dreamed about—and bring an end to April,
straining their elbows, arms and wrists
and every hour closing in on May;

now, with their fingers not quite open yet,
before their thickening green arcade
comes shouldering April away, already I
see in the green a shadow—a regret
that, gaining these few yards of shade,
we lose a mile of cold blue open sky.

Fire

I'd like to get a flame to weave
reliably around a log,

as neatly as a young retriever
jumps and fetches—holds a stick—
docile, like a well-schooled dog.

I'd like the fire to answer fast
when I command. I'd like the flame
to jump and fetch and know its master—
then, when once it starts to lick
the wood, to be not only tame
but steady, neither blaze nor flicker:

Watch the bounding dog, however!
No two leaps are quite the same.

A Simple Thing

A branch that broke with the weight of the winter snow
went on with April, blooming anyway,
its death not having reached its hasty bud.
How simple—not to stop or think or know;
to answer a single impulse with a drive
that assumes the sap as a habit in the blood;
to carry on with the business of the day
and eat the light and call itself alive.

Autumn Afternoon

Okay, we're sitting here together
in the same September weather.
I'd call this a chilly spot,
but look at you: You're sweating hot— .

which means the single world we share
is two worlds that we can't compare
at all. I get a shivery—
a bloodless—kind of chill, to be
so insulated by a skin
that no one else can travel in.

So far apart, although you're sitting there
inches away; and if two bodies find
such different weather in the common air,
think of the space dividing mind from mind.

Clay and Flame

> Nature . . . has mixed us of clay and flame, of brain and mind.
> *William James*

Up from the mineral mud and ore,
from mildew and bacterium
and mold and thallophyte and spore
to fungus, rust and diatom;
from moss and fern and flowering seed
to coral, fluke and sponge, and from
flatworm and snail and centipede
to fish to swamp, until we come
to mouse, to monkey—to the brain
that grew in tandem with the thumb:
To tell exactly how we came
from clay is easy. But explain
the place inside the cranium
where all that clay turns into flame.

Airplane

Now, as you board the airplane, is there latent
in its thorax—nestled near the spine—
some wiring awry, a hose not tightened?
Embolisms inching up the fuel line?
One loose part that's starting to abrade
a second part—a third—without a sign
that some essential fabric's growing frayed?
Or else, in *you*, does some flaw undermine

(undiagnosed) the operation of
the force—and the fragility—that arcs
from fingertip to fingertip above
us on the Sistine ceiling? Let one spark
misfire, and the oxygen won't move
to fire the lungs and drive the heart that bears
you up . . . Now as we stand so hale in love,
some valve is rotting, some small linchpin wears

that holds some cotter pin, mechanics err,
a bolt corrodes; a radon plume delivers
traces to some deficient gene. A mere
omission, fissure, mist can stop whatever
keeps you above the ground: What engineer
invented a machine so frail its breath
depends on something casual as the air
you cruise on, asymptotic to your death?

Scope

A mouse, out there, is quite oblivious
of everything but furry meadow tasks,

the small impedimenta of a world
bounded by roots and grass.

But not the hawk—who apprehends the air,
his own blue field, and, equally, the lower
brown domain of mice—and who's aware
that watching equals power.

I know the field; I know the air. I hold
a hundred hawk-dominions, in a see
unguessed by hawks. So much intelligence!
Enough acuity

to wonder if, outside my own existence,
a watcher at some window watches me.

Photo by Alfred Lippincott

Rachel Wetzsteon was born in New York City in 1967. She is the author of three collections of poems—*The Other Stars* (Penguin, 1994), *Home and Away* (Penguin, 1998), and *Sakura Park* (Persea, 2006)—as well as the forthcoming collection *Silver Roses* (Persea, 2010) and a critical study of W. H. Auden. The recipient of awards from the National Poetry Series, the Ingram Merrill Foundation, and the American Academy of Arts and Letters, she teaches at William Paterson University and lives in Manhattan.

Pemberley

The park was very large. We drove
for some time through a beautiful wood
until the wood ceased, and the house came into view.
Inside were miniatures, small faces
we gawked at until a housekeeper showed us
the master's finer portrait in an upper room.
I dredged up a shaming moment:
you asked me a question, then ducked as I spewed
an idiot's vitriol, blindness disguised as rage.
The house stood well on rising ground,
and beneath its slopes the thirsty couples
held their glasses high at Café Can't Wait.
I spent time at its flimsy tables
but then I walked under trees whose leaves
exhaled gusty stories of good deeds;
I learned empty houses are excellent teachers;
I sent you away and felt you grow
tremendous in your absence. Ask me again.

Gusts

An agitation shakes the trees:
this tumult always seemed to me
the oldest motion, the turbulence
all others copied. As blossoms drift
down through the moist air, so blessings come
to those who wait long enough; when
pollen falls, the flight recalls
a fragile friendship dying. I never thought
that when petals touch the ground
the plenitude might stop there, the fragrance

be neither portent nor memory, but only
sweet smells lasting as long as the walk home.
It is spring; flowers are flying everywhere.
And all night a low voice chides me
for never giving my all to the moment;
a question forms and grows urgent
and won't take no answer for an answer:
if I gave up stories, what would become
of the gust, and the scatter, and the stillness after?
Would the trees be robbed of what made them priceless
or let their riches loose as never before?

Largo

> Look for someone to make you slow.
>
> *Elias Canetti*

They are ogling the stars in an outdoor garden,
and the night's infectious energy
makes them bold, makes him grab her hands and declare
A brilliant chapter begins tonight:
I have novels in me, whole realms of feeling
your eyes prise open. To which she responds
I'm a changeling, darling, in your masterful hands;
this morning I was one of eight million stories
but now I'm wearing freshwater pearls
at the end of a pier, in the middle of summer—
race me there, and the waves will envy our speed.

A sudden hush descends over Café Largo
and a low voice whispers, Be all these things,
ring all these changes on each other
but slowly. The brain that races tonight
will end up a frowning skull in a viewless mansion;

The Swallow Anthology of New American Poets

you'll wake up in bare rooms, horrible jewels in your hands.
Walk, instead, past never-finished cathedrals;
light one cigarette from another;
find, if you know what's good for you, endless answers to whether
the table is really there when you close your eyes.

Love and Work

In an uncurtained room across the way
a woman in a tight dress paints her lips
a deeper red, and sizes up her hips
for signs of ounces gained since yesterday.

She has a thoughtful and a clever face,
but she is also smart enough to know
the truth: however large the brain may grow,
the lashes and the earrings must keep pace.

Although I've spread my books in front of me
with a majestic air of *I'll show her,*
I'm much less confident than I'd prefer,
and now I've started pacing nervously.

I'm poring over theorems, tomes and tracts.
I'm getting ready for a heavy date
by staying up ridiculously late.
But a small voice advises, Face the facts:

go on this way and you'll soon come to harm.
The world's most famous scholars wander down
the most appalling alleyways in town,
a blond and busty airhead on each arm.

There is an inner motor known as lust
that makes a man of learning walk a mile
to gratify his raging senses, while
the woman he can talk to gathers dust.

A chilling vision of the years ahead
invades my thoughts, and widens like a stain:
a barren dance card and a teeming brain,
a crowded bookcase and an empty bed . . .

What if I compromised? I'd stay up late
to hone my elocutionary skills,
and at the crack of dawn I'd swallow pills
to calm my temper and control my weight,

but I just can't. Romantics, so far gone
they think their lovers live for wisdom, woo
by growing wiser; when I think of you
I find the nearest lamp and turn it on.

Great gods of longing, watch me as I work
and if I sprout a martyr's smarmy grin
please find some violent way to do me in;
I'm burning all these candles not to shirk

a night of passion, but to give that night
a richly textured backdrop when it comes.
The girl who gets up from her desk and dumbs
her discourse down has never seen the flight

of wide-eyed starlings from their shabby cage;
the fool whose love is truest is the one

who knows a lover's work is never done.
I'll call you when I've finished one more page.

A Pre-Raphaelite Girlhood

Framed by russet curls, willowy as lilies
tended by the moon, she made bitter tears seem
so sublime that for a long time she was a
flattering mirror

into which I gazed, craving confirmation,
goals, reflections, rules: *I contain a world of*
maladies too good for the world, the canvas
sighed to me softly.

But that was before I compared corollas
of red hair and counted grey eyes and realized
They all look the same. Weakness has a power;
sorrowful maidens

haunt you, there's no way to deny it, with their
noli-me-tangere appeal; but when you
picture them on open-air walks, you sense they'd
melt in a minute.

Rows and rows of ravishing famished creatures,
swooning in Tate Galleries of the brain, still
lift their tragic arms to the waiting clouds and
tempt me to join them,

but I can't come—trudging down muddy roads, I'm
getting my feet dirty to clear my head, I'm

sunlit, breathless, looking for better ways of
looking in mirrors.

On Leaving the Bachelorette Brunch

Because I gazed out the window at birds
doing backflips when the subject turned
to diamonds, because my eyes glazed over
with the slightly sleepy sheen your cake will wear,

never let it be said that I'd rather be
firing arrows at heart-shaped dartboards
or in a cave composing polyglot puns.
I crave, I long for transforming love

as surely as leaves need water and mouths seek bread.
But I also fear the colder changes
that lie in wait and threaten to turn
moons of honey to pools of molasses,

broad front porches to narrow back gardens,
and tight rings of friendship to flimsy things
that break when a gold band brightly implies
Leave early, go home, become one with the one

the world has told you to tend and treasure
above all others. You love, and that's good;
you are loved, that's superb; you will vanish
and reap some happy rewards. But look at the birds.

Madeleine for a While

After Hitchcock's *Vertigo*

Scottie looked down from a very great height,
and as Midge sat primly at her easel
he talked himself back into wholeness:
"I look up, I look down, I look up, I look . . ."

As Midge sat primly at her easel
he followed Madeleine through the city.
"I look up, I look down, I look up, I look . . ."
Down he fell all over again.

He followed Madeleine through the city;
the ghost of mad Carlotta steered her.
Down he fell all over again:
she jumped in the water and he jumped after.

The ghost of mad Carlotta steered her:
"There's someone within me, and she says I must die."
She jumped in the water and he jumped after;
they kissed in the shade of ancient sequoias.

"There's someone within me, and she says I must die."
Haunted Madeleine mounted the steps.
They kissed in the shade of ancient sequoias,
they parted when she leaped from the tower.

Haunted Madeleine mounted the steps;
Scottie pursued, obsessed and dizzy.
They parted when she leaped from the tower,
they met again in a crowded rush hour.

Rachel Wetzsteon   289

Scottie pursued, obsessed and dizzy.
An ill-lit corridor led to her room.
They met again in a crowded rush hour;
they argued in her fleabag hotel.

An ill-lit corridor led to her room;
Judy's dark hair confused the picture.
They argued in her fleabag hotel.
"Be Madeleine for a while," he begged.

Judy's dark hair confused the picture,
ruining the marvelous story.
"Be Madeleine for a while," he begged,
so she returned a dazzling blonde.

Ruining the marvelous story,
her necklace revealed all she had been
when she returned a dazzling blonde.
Holding Madeleine, he'd embraced air.

Her necklace revealed all she had been:
a stumble, a wail, a plunge into darkness.
Holding Madeleine, he'd embraced air.
One final thing and he would be free.

A stumble, a wail, a plunge into darkness.
He talked himself back into wholeness:
one final thing and he would be free.
Scottie looked down from a very great height.

Short Ode to Screwball Women

On sullen nights like these
when my spirit counts its woes like pearls on a string,
you bring me armfuls of spare pantsuits
and clear-eyed hints about the woman
who might kick up her heels in them, flooding rooms
with cunning, air, an almost gaudy vitality.

Gaudy but sober: when your wayward husband
courted the heiress, you stormed her gates
disguised as a floozy—and asked the butler
to serve you ginger-ale. It was life
you'd rather be drunk on, roaring life
that told you there is no time for spirits
of dark staircases, only lightning ruses
that not only leave no bruises but give
all parties their wish: rinsed vision and second chances.

Losing a boot heel and giddily claiming
I was born on the side of a hill is easy.
For every such moment there are ten
when my ideal snags mid-flight, a bag caught in branches.
But a girl can dream, can realize, high
on heroines, that she is mortal
and therefore fearless; that sanity
supplies the ground bass to the wildest singing;
that breezes made visible make the finest winds.

Greg Williamson was born in Columbus, Ohio, in 1964 and raised in Nashville, Tennessee. His three books of poems are *A Most Marvelous Piece of Luck* (Waywiser, 2008), *Errors in the Script* (Overlook, 2001), and *The Silent Partner* (Story Line, 1995). He has received an Academy Award in Literature from the American Academy of Arts and Letters, a fellowship from the National Endowment for the Arts, a Whiting Writers' Award, and the Nicholas Roerich Poetry Prize, among others. He lives in Duluth, Georgia, and teaches in The Writing Seminars at Johns Hopkins University.

Outbound

> We live life forwards and think
> about it backwards.
>
> *Howard Nemerov*

We passengers ride backward on the train
And train our eyes on what has passed us by.
    A cobalt blur composes
    Into a woman picking roses,
Who is already fading in the pane
As in the failing hindsight of the eye.

A line of oaks comes into focus, fades,
Supplanted by the double-dagger poles
    Of power companies,
    Footnotes that redefine the trees.
An asterisk in glass, then window shades,
Graffiti, billboards, tattered banderoles

Of southbound birds. . . . Whatever comes to view
Corrects the view, but never will explain
    The random next event
    Or anything but where we went,
Where long ago a woman wearing blue
Began forgetting someone on a train.

Italics, Mine

Hello, up there. Thank God you happened by.
    I'm touched. I've been beneath the covers
    For so long now the light is stark,
Where honestly I thought that I might lie
    Alone forever in the dark,
    And this is a place for lovers.

Greg Williamson

By night I dreamed about the day you looked
      And read my thoughts and would agree
    To spend some time with me, and talk.
Since all the flights to Paris have been booked,
     Perhaps you'd settle for a walk
      To see what we shall see.

You see that oak leaf there? I always sense
      A kinship with the leaves. To me
    Each one portrays a little oak,
A fragile replica of an immense
     Black oak, itself a lush, baroque,
      Green forest of a tree.

And at the shore let's walk the water line,
      The ocean's flexing, outermost
    Advance, where the seawater laps
A sandy beach, plotting a jagged line
     Whose every subdivision maps
      A continental coast.

Or looking backward toward the mountain range,
      We see the ridge line's collarbone,
    Comprising summit and ravine,
And holding up a rock we find a strange,
     Profound affinity between
      The mountains and the stone.

If I seem to be beginning to repeat
      Myself, it is because the world
    Repeats itself in hidden laws
Whose figurings and fractals the exegete
     Tries to articulate because
      In the beginning was the word.

As with the sense of humor in a laugh,
        In every word a poem survives,
    Abundantly rich in ways and means
To build the sentence and the paragraph,
        The rise and fall of little scenes,
        The stories of our lives.

The coming home of walks and talks and stories
        Discloses what we came to know,
    Where the changing fortunes of a day
Became a lifetime's sadnesses and glories,
        A stranger's face to which we say,
        As to the mirror, "Hello."

Hello. I hope you pardon my conceits,
        But I have dreamed on my nightstands
    From all these little rooms to build
A home where we might lie between the sheets,
        And I declare myself fulfilled
        When I am in your hands.

But this has all been talk, I know, and I
        Can tell you are about to turn
    And go your way, while I repair
To darkness and a dateless night. Goodbye.
        I will be saying a silent prayer
        That one day you return.

The Dial Tone

        They had a bad connection, and the static
            Crackled like gravel drives

Or like the sharp, erratic
Snapping of twigs among dry leaves. Their lives

Had come to this, conducted across long
       Distances. No wonder,
       She said, it all went wrong;
The heart grows firm, but it does not grow fonder,

And she who had once been so hung up on him
       Hung up on him. The phone
       Went dead, and in the dim
Quiescent living room the dial tone

Hummed in his ears that it was finally over,
       A droning vacancy
       That promised to last forever,
Like the flat, pulseless line of an E.K.G.

In which their conversation, their romance,
       This life of dull routine
       And random circumstance
Were merely interruptions on the screen.

From Double Exposures

XIV. Medical School Skeleton with Dominoes Pizza Man

       Superbowl XXX. And see, strung-out and thin,
The skeleton has been exposed against
              The Dominoes Pizza man, enveloped in
A black felt background. Poor Bones, he's been flensed.
              That baggy uniform, a backwards cap,

He's pierced; he's heroin chic; but he's all grins,
        Come from the darkness in his rattletrap,
Burlesquer, rake, this rack of candlepins,
        Giving long odds, right here at the front door,
A real smoothie, with a faint ennui,
        And winning the bet he'll be returning for.
Another working stiff, like you or me.

XV. Profiles: Anne Dancing with Skeleton

        (Or was it XXXI? Oh well.) That's Anne.
And look who's back in this one: portrait style,
        You see, Anne's dancing with the pizza man,
Our old friend Bonesy, with the killer smile,
        Doing a sort of earthy, homegrown bop,
With those dark, bedroom eyes and the cleft chin,
        Belting it out like soul with ZZ Top,
But think about his humble origin,
        Buoyant with life, *jouissance*, the growing buzz
About tough prizes won along the way
        And toasted. But, then, everybody was.
Becoming much the man you see today.

The Life and Times of Wile E. Coyote, Super Genius

    I am a genius by trade.
        W. E. Coyote

With you afling, afang, not yet nonplussed,
Nemesis Roadrunner, Swift-footed, Taker-of-three-
Forks, strange kinetic fellow, animated
Character, that plumed cuckoo, Bird
Thou never wert, sticks out his tongue, waves, peels

Out, and you wrap up a pileated
Bust of smoke. And now? What now? "I must
Dream up a *bril*liant master strategy,

Ingenious, *daring*." Here's to you, Coyote.
Here's to Giant Fly Traps, Quick-Dry Cements,
To ACME Robots, glues, kites, keyhole saws,
DO-IT-YOURSELF TORNADOS, female bird
Impersonations, anvils, Earthquake Pills, . . .
And to the selective repeal of natural laws,
Schemus Backfiribus, a reverse Quixote:
Art turns to mere truth, what it represents,

Then, proven to be true, it turns fictitious.
Roadrunner goes right over the painted span,
You fall to the canyon floor, and from the phony
Tunnel comes the train, *engineered by the bird*,
Your foison, fantasy, feather in your cap,
The better life, your failure—like my own.
Wile E. Everyman. Come, Trickster, let us
Feast on our clay chicken, our tin can.

Binocular Diplopia

> I've tried, Lord knows,
> To keep from seeing double . . .
>
> *James Merrill*

Life was a blur. Or so he thought. The thing
Was, he'd been diagnosed with a small-time
Astigmatism. Why think otherwise?
But when the doctor told him, "Read the chart,"
And he replied, "Which one?" even the smart

Young nurse said, "Uh oh." As for him, his eyes
Were opened and he saw, for the first time,
That he was seeing two of everything.

This would explain a lot. In stereoscopic
Hindsight he reviewed old patterns of
Mistakes: missed shots, a lifetime of misreading,
Mixed signals (this as the nurse was double-knitting
Her cute brows), false moves, smashed thumbs from hitting
The wrong nail on the head, all finally leading
To how the woman he first fell in love
With turned to myth. But that's anther topic.

Meanwhile, the long walk home. Or rather two.
A second one appeared to levitate,
Illusive, epiphanic, and oblique—
Like dual reflections in a double pane
Of glass, or some self-referential strain
Of allegory. Which one, so to speak,
Was true? If seeing's believing, not the great
Sam Johnson could refute it: Both were true.

Twinned like a postcard's double-stamped cachet,
The phone lines added up to musical staves,
With a score of birds; Shell's logo seemed to shine
Like a big con; and everywhere he turned,
His second nature brazenly returned
Equivocations in the plainest sign,
From the fiduciary JESUS SAVES
To the unfortunate SLOW CHILDREN AT PLAY,

As if the world were, after all, a text,
"A book in folio," a hieroglyph.

Here was the uncorrected proof. The elder's
Two thick volumes of belated leaves
And, spiraling in double helices,
Its legendary keys all seemed to tell,
Beside themselves, another tale, as if

These traces were the cryptic analects
Of some long-lost original. (Or flimflam!
Now get real. This is pure grandstanding.
Look in thy heart, etc.) Double trouble.
Even close introspection was abased.
With two left feet, twin-featured and two-faced,
He saw, head down, foreshortened in a puddle,
Under a critical sign that said, NO STANDING,
Me. (When was it I turned into him?)

So that was that. And he (we'll say) set out
Again, flung open the double doors to find
Her smiling faces, whom he'd fancied for
So long as muse, and girl back home, and quest,
And so much more. Closing his eyes to rest
He saw her image turn from metaphor
To perfect vision, singular, clear, defined,
The one thing he had always dreamt about.

Time

For John Hollander

Time was, it wasn't. "Then," a singularity,
Planck's constant, quantum foam, the bottom quark—
Better let them tell it—and, presto, we
Had time. Thus, gnomons, Stonehenge, Harrison's clock.

Time had a future. Time was *in!* And you
Could make it, save it, spend it, even un-
derestimate it (time is money, son?
Sure, but this ain't the time your father knew)

Until your limo slides up to the high
Society grand ball, everyone's there,
Tripping the tarantella ("*merci*, with lime")
The old soft shoe, high hat, a final air
Under the milky way, the signs, the sky-
light's stars, where everything is done

                              in time.

Fire

Imagine that first fire, the doubletakes
Among the vegans, cold, dark, wet: Cave guy
Strikes flint and, boom, you're grilling mammoth steaks,
You're holding hands, you're hooking up, you're dry,

And (years of R&D) it catches on,
Brick ovens, candlelight, of course appalling
Losses, but still, fondue, filet mignon,
And the three-alarm, fanned fire of your first calling

Until there's no more call for you, you box
Up your life's work, archive the ardencies,
The once hot, test-tube topics, and retire
To country climes, keeping an eye on the phlox
In your old field, avuncular now, at peace
With not quite having set the world

                              on fire.

CHRISTIAN WIMAN

Photo by Robert Murphy

Christian Wiman was born in Abilene, Texas, in 1966. His books of poetry are *The Long Home* (Story Line, 1998; Copper Canyon, 2005) and *Hard Night* (Copper Canyon, 2005). His collection of essays, *Ambition and Survival: Becoming a Poet* (Copper Canyon), appeared in 2007. He is the editor of *Poetry* and lives in Chicago.

Hard Night

What words or harder gift
does the light require of me
carving from the dark
this difficult tree?

What place or farther peace
do I almost see
emerging from the night
and heart of me?

The sky whitens, goes on and on.
Fields wrinkle into rows
of cotton, go on and on.
Night like a fling of crows
disperses and is gone.

What song, what home,
what calm or one clarity
can I not quite come to,
never quite see:
this field, this sky, this tree.

Dream of a Dead Friend

When the world was merely beautiful
And talk was keeping us from speech;
When the walk was almost over
And we were still just out of reach,
You closed my eyes

And led me by the hand
Through brush and low branches to stand
In the deep snow.

That cold was something I could feel.
That darkness was a choice.
Though I couldn't see your face
I could hear your voice
Describe a sky
And a fine-needled pine tree,
A field, and snow, and you, and me.
Then you let go.

If I say the world is real
And outside my window is a dawn;
If I say the proof of love is grief
And trees are greener being gone,
Why, oh why
Will none of this be true
But in the moment I reach for you
Saying *no, no*.

Clearing

It was when I walked lost
in the burn and rust
of late October that I turned
near dusk toward the leaf-screened
light of a green clearing in the trees.
In the untracked and roadless open
I saw an intact but wide open house,

half-standing and half-lost
to unsuffered seasons of wind
and frost: warped tin and broken stone,
old wood combed by the incurious sun.
The broad wall to the stark north,
each caulked chink and the solid hearth
dark with all the unremembered fires
that in the long nights quietly died,
implied a life of bare solitude
and hardship, little to hold
and less to keep, aching days
and welcome sleep in the mind-clearing cold.
And yet the wide sky, the wildflowered ground
and the sound of the wind
in the burn and rust of late October
as the days shortened and the leaves turned
must have been heartening, too,
to one who walked out of the trees
into a green clearing that he knew.
If you could find this place,
or even for one moment feel
in the word-riddled remnants
of what I felt there
the mild but gathering air, see the leaves
that with one good blast would go,
you could believe
that standing in a late weave of light and shade
a man could suddenly want his life,
feel it blaze in him and mean,
as for a moment I believed,
before I walked on.

What I Know

These fields go farther than you think they do.
That darkness is my father walking away.
It is my shadow that I tell this to.

This stillness is not real. The cloud that grew
Into an old man's face didn't stay.
These fields go farther than you think they do.

The sun loves shattered things, and loves what's new.
I love you so much more than I can say.
It is my shadow that I tell this to.

He is not sleeping, that bird the bugs crawl through.
Don't touch. Don't cry. Think good things. Pray
These fields go farther than you think they do.

Some darknesses breathe, look back at you.
Under the porch a pair of eyes waits all day.
It is my shadow that I tell this to.

The things my father told me must be true:
There are some places where you cannot play.
These fields go farther than you think they do.
It is my shadow that I tell this to.

From a Window

Incurable and unbelieving
In any truth but the truth of grieving,

I saw a tree inside a tree
Rise kaleidoscopically

As if the leaves had livelier ghosts.
I pressed my face as close

To the pane as I could get
To watch that fitful, fluent spirit

That seemed a single being undefined
Or countless beings of one mind

Haul its strange cohesion
Beyond the limits of my vision

Over the house heavenwards.
Of course I knew those leaves were birds.

Of course that old tree stood
Exactly as it had and would

(But why should it seem fuller now?)
And though a man's mind might endow

Even a tree with some excess
Of life to which a man seems witness,

That life is not the life of men.
And that is where the joy came in.

Sitting Down to Breakfast Alone

Brachest, she called it, gentling grease
over blanching yolks with an expertise
honed from three decades of dawns

at the Longhorn Diner in Loraine,
where even the oldest in the old men's booth
swore as if it were scripture truth
they'd never had a breakfast better,
rapping a glass sharply to get her
attention when it went sorrowing
so far into some simple thing—
the jangly door or a crusted pan,
the wall clock's black, hitchy hands—
that she would startle, blink, then grin
as if discovering them all again.
Who remembers now when one died
the space that he had occupied
went unfilled for a day, then two, three,
until she unceremoniously
plunked plates down in the wrong places
and stared their wronged faces
back to banter she could hardly follow.
Unmarried, childless, homely, "slow,"
she knew coffee cut with chamomile
kept the grocer Paul's ulcer cool,
yarrow in gravy eased the islands
of lesions in Larry Borwick's hands,
and when some nightlong nameless urgency
made him seek some human company
Brother Tom needed hash-browns with cheese.
She knew to nod at the litany of cities
the big-rig long-haulers bragged her past,
to laugh when the hunters asked
if she'd pray for them or for the quail
they went laughing off to kill,
and then—envisioning one

rising so fast it seemed the sun
tugged at it—to do exactly that.
Who remembers where they all sat:
crook-backed builders, drought-faced farmers,
VF'ers muttering through their wars,
night-shift roughnecks so caked in black
it seemed they made their way back
every morning from the dead.
Who remembers one word they said?
The Longhorn Diner's long torn down,
the gin and feedlots gone, the town
itself now nothing but a name
at which some bored boy has taken aim,
every letter light-pierced and partial.
Sister, Aunt Sissy, Bera Thrailkill,
I picture you some dime-bright dawn
grown even brighter now for being gone
bustling amid the formica and chrome
of that small house we both called home
during the spring that was your last.
All stories stop: once more you are lost
in something I can merely see:
steam spiriting out of black coffee,
the scorched pores of toast, a bowl
of apple butter like edible soil,
bald cloth, knifelight, the lip of a glass,
my plate's gleaming, teeming emptiness . . .

Late Fragment

How to say this—
my silences were not always mine:

scrabbled hole and the dark beyond,
vaporous pond
as if water wanted out of itself,
tip of the sycamore's weird bare reach:
some latency in things leading not so much to speech
as to a halting, haunted art
wherein to master was to miss—
how to say this, how to say this . . .

My father was a boatbuilder.
Prow of a man, his world a sea to cleave.
I learned a dangerous patience,
to navigate night, live on nothing, leave.
And my mother, her furious smallness,
her way of saying her blade, the oil and onion's hiss:
from her I learned what lies beneath.

Mystic, Istanbul, Jakarta, Dar es Salaam—
what was I meant to keep?
If the distances to which I've been given
suggest some wantless heaven
of the mind, what in me still traces
the creekbed creases
in the rough skin of the palm
of one so long, long asleep?

If I say I loved the seagull
tethered to its cry, the cypress's imprisoned winds,
speak to the brink of my hands
a moss-covered rock
soft and knobby as a kitten's skull.
If I say I loved.

Boston, Cardiff, Lisbon, Asunción:
what name is not a horizon?
Somewhere it is evening,
light grown mild and pliable,
wielded by wave and rock,
in the shore's trees torn apart . . .

MARK WUNDERLICH

Photo by Mary Jane Dean

Mark Wunderlich was born in 1968 in Winona, Minnesota, and grew up in Fountain City, Wisconsin. He is the author of *The Anchorage* (University of Massachusetts Press, 1999), which received the Lambda Literary Award, and *Voluntary Servitude* (Graywolf, 2004). He is the recipient of a Wallace Stegner Fellowship from Stanford University and two fellowships from the Fine Arts Work Center in Provincetown, as well as fellowships from the National Endowment for the Arts and the Massachusetts Cultural Council. He has taught in the graduate writing programs of Columbia University, Sarah Lawrence College, and Ohio University and currently teaches literature and writing at Bennington College in Vermont. He lives in Catskill, New York.

From a Vacant House

It is hard to want a thing you know will hurt another,
yet the heart persists, doesn't it, with its dark urges, liquid wish?

A sea town. Gulls, those malefica, uselessly scissor
thin-boned bodies against a beach washed of its will,

where a season ago women lay, dogs and children fastened
to the long arms of their concern, the men vacant and glittery

with spandex and oil. It is November, and already books thicken
at my bedside, a crush of paper characters awaiting the eye's

hurried pass, their unread stories attendant through the night,
until its bandage lifts to a morning blush, and I am held

within the parenthesis of a spare white house, a little thinner,
empty hands chilled like the faithful, offering myself to discipline's

cool machinery. I will stand on the pier, gesturing and cold.
I will open my mouth to your opening mouth.

Take Good Care of Yourself

On the runway at the Roxy, the drag queen
fans herself gently, but with purpose.
She is an Asian princess, an elaborate wig
jangling like bells on a Shinto temple,
shoulders broad as my father's. With a flick

of her fan she covers her face, a whole
world of authority in that one gesture,
a screen sliding back, all black lacquer
and soprano laugh. The music in this place
echoes with the whip-crack of 2,000

men's libidos, and the one bitter pill
of X-tasy dissolving on my tongue is the perfect
slender measure of the holy ghost,
the vibe crawling my spine exactly,
I assure myself, what I've always wanted.

It is 1992. There is no *you* yet for me
to address, just simple imperative. *Give*
me more. Give. It is a vision, I'm sure
of this, of what heaven might provide—a sea
of men all muscle, white briefs and pearls,

of kilts cut too short for Catholic girls
or a Highland fling. Don't bother with chat
just yet. I've stripped and checked my shirt
at the door. I need a drink, a light, someplace
a little cooler, just for a minute, to chill.

There is no place like the unbearable ribbon
of highway that cuts the Midwest into two unequal
halves, a pale sun glowing like the fire
of one last cigarette. It is the prairie
I'm scared of, barreling off in all directions

flat as its inhabitants' A's and O's. I left
Wisconsin's well-tempered rooms
and snow-fields white and vacant as a bed
I wish I'd never slept in. Winters
I stared out the bus window through frost

at an icy template of what the world offered up—
the moon's tin cup of romance and a beauty,
that if held too long to the body
would melt. If I felt anything for you then
it was mere, the flicker of possibility

a quickening of the pulse when I imagined
a future, not here but elsewhere, the sky
not yawning out, but hemmed in. In her dress
the drag is all glitter and perfect grace,
pure artifice, beating her fan, injuring

the smoky air, and in the club, I'm still
imagining. The stacks of speakers burn
and throb, whole cities of sound bear down
on us. I'm dancing with men all around me,
moving every muscle I can, the woman's voice

mixed and extended to a gorgeous black note
is a song that only now can I remember—
one familiar flat stretch, one wide-open vista
and a rhythm married to words
for what we still had to lose.

Difficult Body

A story: There was a cow in the road, struck by a semi—
half-moon of carcass and jutting legs, eyes
already milky with dust and snow, rolled upward

as if tired of this world tilted on its side.
We drove through the pink light of the police cruiser,
her broken flank blowing steam in the air.

Minutes later, a deer sprang onto the road
and we hit her, crushed her pelvis—the drama reversed,
first consequence, then action—but the doe,

not dead, pulled herself with front legs
into the ditch. My father went to her, stunned her
with a tire iron before cutting her throat, and today I think

of the body of St. Francis in the Arizona desert,
carved from wood and laid in his casket,
lovingly dressed in red and white satin

covered in petitions—medals, locks of hair,
photos of infants, his head lifted and stroked,
the grain of his brow kissed by the penitent.

O wooden saint, dry body. I will not be like you,
carapace. A chalky shell scooped of its life.
I will leave less than this behind me.

Amaryllis

After Rilke

You've seen a cat consume a hummingbird,
scoop its beating body from the pyracantha bush
and break its wings with tufted paws
before marshalling it, whole, into its bone-tough throat;
seen a boy, heart racing with cocaine, climb
from a car window to tumble on the ground,
his search for pleasure ending in skinned palms;
heard a woman's shouts as she is pushed into the police cruiser,
large hand pressing her head into the door,
red lights spinning their tornado in the street.

But all of that will fade; on the table is the amaryllis
pushing its monstrous body in the air,
requiring no soil to do so, having wound
two seasons' rot into a white and papered bulb,
exacting nutrition from the winter light,
culling from complex chemistry the tints
and fragments that tissue and pause and build

again the pigment and filament.
The flower crescendos toward the light,
though better to say despite it,
gores through gorse and pebble
to form a throat—so breakable—open
with its tender pistils, damp with rosin,
simple in its simple sex, to burn and siphon
itself in air. Tongue of fire, tongue
of earth, the amaryllis is a rudiment
forming its meretricious petals
to trumpet and exclaim.

How you admire it. It vibrates
in the draft, a complex wheel
bitten with cogs, swelling and sexual
though nothing will touch it. You forced it
to spread itself, to cleave and grasp,
remorseless, open to your assignments—
this is availability, this is tenderness,
this red plane is given to the world.
Sometimes the heart breaks. Sometimes
it is not held hostage. The red world
where cells prepare for the unexpected
splays open at the window's ledge.
But not human you inhuman thing.
No anxious, no foible, no hesitating hand.
Pry with fiber your course through sand.
Point your whole body toward the unknown
away from the dead.
Be water and light and land—
no contrivance, no gasp, no dream
where there is no head.

Mark Wunderlich   317

Lamb

Inside the sheep's hot center, lambs tangle,
soft joints press a tender twin.

I am brought to the barn, soap my arm in a sink.
Orion stabs the sky with his arrow of ice.

I unwrap one sister from her awakening sister,
carefully, for the flesh is tender and this is an animal will.

Hand in the cave where blood shapes into an other,
I will bring them forth, bleating into January.

Good shepherd, I will shelter them from fangs,
chase stray dogs with a gun, turn them onto grass in spring.

They will come when I call, press against woven wire
even though I call them to the gleaming hook.

Tack

Bridle and martingale,
the crupper's strap and buckle,

hobble and tassel binds
the mare to matter. Crack

of the crop's split flap on a flank.
Push begged the animal,

Push begged the man
and the two sprang out,

half-moon of mud flung
from a hoof. Finger flick,

check bit, metal on the tongue
leather in the hand,

knee turned to saddle girdle,
girth gives a little, looser.

Speed is the animal
wish is the man—

curve the neck, roll the eye
the jump is high

but will is all. Pull
strap, fit thigh,

skin covers muscle,
matter is the mind.

The Buck

I shot the buck and he crumpled,

folded like a ladder into the snow.

He had bounded along a worn path,

jumped a fallen log and paused,

turning his flank toward me

and I saw his nostrils flare

through the ocular concentration

of a rifle's scope. I placed the red bead

of the sight on the fur covering the spot

above the twin bellows of his lungs,

and squeezed the trigger to release the shot.

There was a pause after the rifle's report

during which my heart and the buck's surged,

though only mine would propel me into a future,

in which I bore a knife and numerous pockets,

carried a lanyard that I would lash

to the buck's antler rack and drag him

down a logging road to the stubbled field.

>*Why did you shoot the deer?*

Because we were hunting.

>*Did you enjoy it? The hunting?*

I'm not sure. I think I did.

>*I mean, did you enjoy it when you killed?*

Yes.

>*What was enjoyable?*

I was powerful. I could put an end to something independent.

>*That's an enjoyable thing?*

No. Something changes, just before the fatal moment.

>*Yes? What changed?*

I saw the future.

DAVID YEZZI

David Yezzi was born in Albany, New York, in 1966. His books of poetry are *The Hidden Model* (TriQuarterly Books/Northwestern University Press, 2003) and *Azores* (Swallow/Ohio University Press, 2008). His libretto for a chamber opera by David Conte, *Firebird Motel*, received its world premiere in San Francisco in 2003 and was released on CD in 2007. From 1998 to 2000, he was a Stegner Fellow in poetry at Stanford University. A former director of the Unterberg Poetry Center of the 92nd Street Y, he is executive editor of the *New Criterion*. He lives in New York City.

The Call

The call comes and you're out. When you retrieve
the message and return the call, you learn
that someone you knew distantly has died.
His bereaved partner takes you through the news.

She wants to tell you personally how
he fought and, then, how suddenly he went.
She's stunned, and you feel horrible for her,
though somewhat dazed, since he was not a friend,

just someone you saw once or twice a year,
and who, in truth, always produced a shudder:
you confess that you never liked him much,
not to her, of course, but silently to yourself.

You feel ashamed, or rather think the word
ashamed, and hurry off the line. That's when
the image of him appears more vividly,
with nicotine-stained fingertips and hair

like desert weeds fetched up on chicken wire,
the rapacious way he always buttonholed
you at a launch, his breath blowsy with wine.
Well, that will never ever happen again:

one less acquaintance who stops to say hello,
apparently happy at the sight of you.
So why then this surprising queasiness,
not of repulsion but of something like remorse

that comes on you without your guessing it,
till the thing that nagged you most—his laugh, perhaps—

becomes the very music that you miss,
or think you do, or want to, now he's gone.

Free Period

> Outside study hall,
it's me, my girlfriend, and a guy
named Rob—bony kid, klutzy
at games, fluent in French.
> He's behind her;

> I'm asleep or half-
asleep (it's morning), and, as I
squint into the trapezoid of light
breaking on the bench and me,
> I see him raise

> his hand to her head
from the back, so gently
she doesn't notice
him at first, but stands there,
> carved in ebony

> and beaten gold:
Stacey's straight black hair
falling in shafts of sun.
He smoothes it down,
> firmly now,

> so that she turns,
kind of freaked, as if to say,
"Can you believe it?"

to me still coming to.
       Yes, I guess I can,

      I think to myself,
with only a twinge
of jealousy, with admiration,
actually. And pity—since he'd
      seen beauty raw,

      for which humiliation
was the smallest price,
and, dazzled, grasped at it,
not getting hold.
      It wasn't his, god knows,

      or mine, as I,
months later, learned
hopelessly—almost fatally,
it felt—or even hers, though it was
      of her and around her,

      in that freeze-frame
of low sunshine,
with us irremediably young
and strung-out from love
      and lack of love.

The Good News

      A friend calls, so I ask him to stop by.
We sip old Scotch, the good stuff, order in,
some Indian—no frills too fine for him

or me, particularly since it's been
        ages since we made the time.

    Two drinks in, we've caught up on our plans.
I've sleepwalked through the last few years by rote;
he's had a nasty rough patch, quote-unquote,
on the home front. So, we commiserate,
        cupping our lowballs in our hands.

    It's great to see him, good to have a friend
who feels the same as you about his lot—
that, while some grass is greener, your small plot
is crudely arable, and though you're not
        so young, it's still not quite the end.

    As if remembering then, he spills his news.
Though I was pretty lit, I swear it's true,
it was as if a gold glow filled the room
and shone on him, a sun-shaft piercing through
        dense clouds, behind which swept long views.

    In that rich light, he looked, not like my friend
but some acquaintance brushed by on the train.
Had his good fortune kept me from the same,
I had to wonder, a zero sum game
        that gave the night its early end?

    Nothing strange. Our drinks were done, that's all.
We haven't spoken since. By morning, I
couldn't remember half of what the guy
had said, just his good news, my slurred goodbye,
        the click of the latch, the quiet hall.

David Yezzi   325

Azores

i

Heeled over on the sea's domed emptiness,
a sail on the horizon slowly yields
its full size, appearing as a shadow, less
a substance than a rumor blown though fields
that the prevailing wind has furrowed white
and black. Now here it is, an hour on.
The sloop has metamorphosed from a kite
drawn on an unseen string, a distant song
the breeze broke up and scattered in our wake,
to a towering spar beneath a charcoal sky,
gaining, massive, on our tiny stern:
an elephant, a senseless lob of strokes,
whose slow approach we patiently discern,
an unintended sharer lying by.

ii

When the last morning lights fade finally—
each foreign sun run roughshod by our own,
which, hoisted up toward noon, looms large, a stone
scattering sparks along a flinty sea—
I am anxious to have them back again,
crowded above the masthead in light wind,
the pole star amber as we crane to find
true north on nights that show no sign of rain.
The memory of them fades in brightened skies,
a secret so refined it cannot brook

the drab unsubtle breeze and public looks
of post meridiem, the way your eyes
spoke candidly to me at first and then
admitted nothing when I looked again.

iii

The vision of a sunset on the ocean:
countless tongues of flame, as if a wood
had roared up just as evening set in motion
its day's-end rituals of neighborhood.
Nearby shelters shudder in the smoke.
In the middle of this fire, there is no reason,
only a vague account of something broken
that we will not miss now—not in this season
of ember-glow and godsent conflagration.
It will be hours on, when the lost light
cools the scene back to sense, that the relation
of what was to what remains will tinge the night
with an acrid fog still clinging in the air
like a manifest of what's no longer there.

iv

If there is one sustaining fact, it's this:
horizon—Manichean anchor of
our darkening half-world, binding the grays above
the main with breaking waves and constant hiss.
Consider for a moment that the line
you gaze along is not the sea and sky,
but sliding forms, a drama for the eye,
a plum disturbance, cello chords, a seine
of drenched debris clogging the world below.

Aloft: a gauzelike exhale and a haze
through which a searchlight sears its blooded rays.

These masses point to nothing we can know.
Perhaps, just this: that it's not possible
to pin the spirit by an act of will.

v

Hove to: the tiller lashed and set against
a backing foresail trimmed to contradict

a strong impulse to fall off from the wind:
two canceling passions, each one meant to end

the other's outsized wish to turn away
and toward: each countermands the other's sway,

until the bow lies flummoxed in the gale,
stunned and bleating, as the rigging flails

and, heaving, we lie on the cabin floor.
This is what it is to live at war:

sleeplessness, recrimination, shame,
rage, paranoia, cleaving, and the name—

like poison—on my lips no longer the same
one I conjured with before the weather came.

vi

The sky this morning—a scar, whose low sun
                    trails breath-shadows over teak,
like Eros flying past on parchment wings
—turns enemy.
                    Our natural state is sickness:
(But, as in sickness, did I loathe this food).

What in the weather changes, such that wind,
which needled us to make our way across
now wants us gone,
                        with no trace remaining
of the hull that held us, or the sails
that bellied, as lungs fill, with the very force
of—not love—but aspiration, at least?
Drowned, who could then point to us and say . . .

　　　vii

The eye, at dawn, finds no significance
or object carved into the marble sea
that a pilot could dead reckon from, the lee
as blank as what's to windward. Slow advance,
as stark division swallows its own heels—
the round horizon ends where it begins,
repeatedly, a cyclorama of winds,
a lens trained on high cloud banks that reveals
nothing but blur.
                        Below, the fleshy swells
charge on like herds scenting some distant cue
to move. They crowd together toward a new
safety, harbored and far from warning bells,
till the last rays of the sun recede, then fail,
again without the sighting of a sail.

　　　viii

The sheets and stays go slack in renewed calm,
and, for the first time in a week, our thoughts
race free above this skin of shallow troughs.
Hardly-moving waves caress the helm,
as the same stream that urged us on for days
now presses to our sides a guileless hand,

David Yezzi

and trade winds peter, free of flux. We stand
unhitching reefs, transfixed by the small ways
sound reasserts itself without the wind:
the gauzy rush of breath, a wheeze of line,
the halyards' endless ticking finally gone
in a warm repose that sunset can't rescind.
We wash ourselves, removing streaks of brine,
new baptized in an hour of halcyon.

ix

A green island draped in volcanic smoke,
imperceptible at first, until the reek
of musk wafts to us seaward over a league,
like the pong of love-sheets a summer night has soaked,
retaining, in the after-dawn, the very smell
that brought the madness on. All this we know
before the misted hills float into view.
The fact of land's not what your dreams foretell.
Its bitter law, a wafer on the tongue:
we are not suited to live long at sea.
Though shoreward-days run down as certainly,
they are a habit that we can't unlearn,
like lines creasing the smooth palm of the hand,
this lust for water, fidelity to land.

C. DALE YOUNG

Photo by Marion Ettlinger

C. Dale Young was born in 1969 and grew up in south Florida. He is the author of three collections of poetry: *The Day Underneath the Day* (Northwestern University Press, 2001), *The Second Person* (Four Way Books, 2007), and *TORN* (Four Way Books, forthcoming 2012). He works full-time as a physician, edits poetry for the *New England Review*, and teaches in the Warren Wilson MFA Program for Writers. He lives in San Francisco.

Torn

There was the knife and the broken syringe
then the needle in my hand, the Tru-Cut
followed by the night-blue suture.

The wall behind registration listed a man
with his face open. Through the glass doors,
I saw the sky going blue to black as it had

24 hours earlier when I last stood there gazing off
into space, into the nothingness of that town.
Bat to the head. Knife to the face. They tore

down the boy in an alleyway, the broken syringe
skittering across the sidewalk. No concussion.
But the face torn open, the blood congealed

and crusted along his cheek. *Stitch up the faggot
in bed 6* is all the ER doctor had said.
Queasy from the lack of sleep, I steadied

my hands as best as I could after cleaning up
the dried blood. There was the needle
and the night-blue suture trailing behind it.

There was the flesh torn and the skin open.
I sat there and threw stitch after stitch
trying to put him back together again.

When the tears ran down his face,
I prayed it was a result of my work
and not the work of the men in the alley.

Even though I knew there were others to be seen,
I sat there and slowly threw each stitch.
There were always others to be seen. There was

always the bat and the knife. I said nothing,
and the tears kept welling in his eyes.
And even though I was told to be "quick and dirty,"

told to spend less than 20 minutes, I sat there
for over an hour closing the wound so that each edge
met its opposing match. I wanted him

to be beautiful again. *Stitch up the faggot in bed 6.*
Each suture thrown reminded me I would never be safe
in that town. There would always be the bat

and the knife, always a fool willing to tear me open
to see the dirty faggot inside. And when they
came in drunk or high with their own wounds,

when they bragged about their scuffles with the knife
and that other world of men, I sat there and sutured.
I sat there like an old woman and sewed them up.

Stitch after stitch, the slender exactness of my fingers
attempted perfection. I sat there and sewed them up.

Recitativo

As an arrow flies through the air, some
will say it swims because it bends and flexes
from side to side, like a fish does, like a fish swims.

But is that true? True, but not exact.
It isn't enough to say the arrow swims.
It isn't enough to say the arrow quivers.

Remember the spine of the arrow is wood.
It cannot be aluminum because such things
were not yet known in that world—the spine
limber enough to avoid the drawn bow's shattering.
Know that the arrow does not serve the bow.
Know that the bow does not serve the arrow.

Not powder blue, but powdery and blue.
Not bound to a tree, but hands strung up to a tree.
Distinctions like these are, in fact, important
when the time comes for you to recount the story.
It isn't enough to say the arrows flew.
It isn't enough to say the arrows pierced.

The turkey doesn't fly nor does it swim.
But its feathers are essential for the arrow
to meet its target. The air is a swarm of arrows
and, for less than a minute, it could be called beautiful.
Know that the arrow, now arrows, will strike the flesh.
Know that the arrows, now arrow, will meet the target.

This is an old story, powdery lens of time having made
the light of it softer, almost as sweet as this music.
You must tell it. You will tell it. The man's head refuses
to slump. It cocks to one side, the eyes refusing to shut.
It isn't enough to say they killed the man.
It is never enough to say he became a saint.

Sepsis

The fog has yet to lift, God, and still the bustle
of buses and garbage trucks. God, I have coveted
sleep. I have wished to find an empty bed

in the hospital while on call. I have placed
my bodily needs first, left nurses to do
what I should have done. And so, the antibiotics

sat on the counter. They sat on the counter
under incandescent lights. No needle was placed
in the woman's arm. No IV was started. It sat there

on the counter waiting. I have coveted sleep, God,
and the toxins I studied in Bacteriology took hold
of Your servant. When the blood flowered

beneath her skin, I shocked her, placed the paddles
on her chest, her dying body convulsing each time.
The antibiotics sat on the counter, and shame

colored my face, the blood pooling in my cheeks
like heat. And outside, the stars continued falling
into place. And the owl kept talking without listening.

And the wind kept sweeping the streets clean.
And the heart in my chest stayed silent.
How could I have known that I would never forget,

that early some mornings, in the waking time,
the fog still filling the avenues, that the image
of her body clothed in sweat would find me?

I have disobeyed my Oath. I have caused harm.
I have failed the preacher from the Baptist Church.
Dear God, how does a sinner outlast the sin?

Or Something Like That

In the Yard today, the pine needles began snowing
down. The way they caught the light was curious.
And the maple's leaves, all red and ochre, were

already littering the walkway. And I, well I sat
thinking the same dark thoughts I have had
since childhood. You know the ones. I need

not explain them to You, of all people.
But it is so easy to call things dark thoughts,
a kind of lazy shorthand. Too easy to forget

the maxim that everyone is good in Your eyes.
We both know this is not true, is a lie. I mean,
the high school counselor they put away for life . . .

How can he be good in Your eyes? Sometimes,
I am convinced no one is good in Your eyes.
Dark thoughts, yes. I am doubting again.

I doubt the pine needles, the maple leaves,
the robin carrying on its stupid song,
my own voice mumbling on a slate blue terrace.

Easy to doubt. Always easy. And the old Jesuit
who lectured me on this? Well, he doubted, too.
But I am not quite ready to be broken just yet.

I have a few things left in me, a few surprises.
No magic is as good as Your magic, but I have
hidden cards up my sleeve, twisted the handkerchief,

slipped the coin behind my watch. I still have
a few tricks left to play. And the light shifting
on the terrace, the pine needles coming down,

I know what they mean. I get what You are trying
to get at. I am here, God, I am here. I am waiting
for You to blind me with a sunstorm of stars.

In the Cutting Room

That the falling glass, the one
that falls 4 feet before shattering
into 18 pieces, is caught in something
between 64 and an infinite number of frames
between edge of table and the kitchen's

fake Italian marble floor. . . . This is exactly
the kind of crap I cannot stand to hear.
God in the details. God in the minutiae
of a falling body, a mass falling
through space and time. What shutter fly genius,

what poet of a scientist discovered this?
I reject the scientific. I have
halted the glass exactly 4 inches
above the ground and reveled in the
"potential" of it. I have halted your heart

exactly 4 inches above the ground. See
how easily I revise our history? See how I
have swapped my heart for your own?
The falling heart about to shatter, held
in space, in time, by the mind's quicker-than-thou

apertures? Exactly the kind of crap I cannot stand.
I have held a heart in my own hands, the heavy
rubbery mass of it slick with blood and saline.
With forceps and dissecting probe, I have
opened each valve, studied its small ears

that sometimes fill with blood. Circumflex,
Left Anterior Descending, I have followed
the pathways blood takes around the heart.
I am not qualified to speak about God and Physick.
I have no gift for the 35-mm world of

quick shutter and quicker thought. Who does?
I speak what I know. I speak with a filthy mouth.
And what do I know? What could I possibly know?
That the heart is tougher than you think. That it
does not break. That it, too, becomes dust.

Inheritance

Long Dead. He had been Long Dead. Such an odd phrase.
How long is Long Dead? How many moons is that?
But my use of the words "many moons" offended
my Great Uncle, who raised his eyebrows and mumbled
that I should stop speaking like a pansy. I did not
know then that flowers could speak. I wasn't old enough.
And I rehearsed the words in my head, repeating them

The Swallow Anthology of New American Poets

with various inflections: many moons, many moons.
And when I tired, I shouted that there was a murder
of crows in the yard. Ah the English sneer, the slight curl
of the upper lip and the flaring of the tight nostrils.
Great Uncle barked something about a gaggle of geese.
And when it was pointed out there were no crows in the yard,
oh the looks, the shaking of heads, the word liar
and, again, pansy. Yes, I was alive by the Grace of God.
By the Grace of God: it sounded so lovely, so pristine.
Grace, that beautiful but difficult thing to divine,
and God, well, God was God. The teacup returned
to its saucer so quickly it broke. The book glided,
like the quickest of jaybirds, into the kitchen window.
What had I said? What could I possibly have said?
That William Richard Extant August would have killed me,
that he should have killed my mother, is all I remember
my Great Uncle shouting. I was not a real man, a man's
man, a man of guts, a pure man, an honorable man.
In the portrait of him near the sunroom, his head tilted
between direct stare and a sly, almost feminine, profile,
there was a mole on the upper inner edge of his left earlobe.
William Richard Extant August, I had never met you.
I had never killed anything with my bare hands.
And years later, having learned to shave, I find it.
There, on my ear, the same mole, in the same spot.
Long Dead? No, not dead at all. Asleep. Resting.
Waiting for the right time to make himself known.

The Bridge

I love. Wouldn't we all like to start
a poem with "I love . . ."? I would.

I mean, I love the fact there are parallel lines
in the word "parallel," love how

words sometimes mirror what they mean.
I love mirrors and that stupid tale
about Narcissus. I suppose
there is some Narcissism in that.

You know, Narcissism, what you
remind me to avoid almost all the time.
Yeah, I love Narcissism. I do.
But what I really love is ice cream.

Remember how I told you
no amount of ice cream can survive
a week in my freezer. You didn't believe me,
did you? No, you didn't. But you know now

how true that is. I love
that you know my Achilles heel
is none other than ice cream—
so chilly, so common.

And I love fountain pens. I mean
I just love them. Cleaning them,
filling them with ink, fills me
with a kind of joy, even if joy

is so 1950. I know, no one talks about
joy anymore. It is even more taboo
than love. And so, of course, I love joy.
I love the way joy sounds as it exits

your mouth. You know, the *word* joy.
How joyous is that. It makes me think
of bubbles, chandeliers, dandelions.
I love the way the mind runs

that pathway from bubbles to dandelions.
Yes, I love a lot. And right here,
walking down this street,
I love the way we make

a bridge, a suspension bridge
—almost as beautiful as the
Golden Gate Bridge—swaying
as we walk hand in hand.

ACKNOWLEDGMENTS

Craig Arnold: "The Singers" first appeared in *Poetry* © 2007 Craig Arnold. "Cedar Waxwings" first appeared in *Yale Review* © 2009 Craig Arnold. "Uncouplings" first appeared in *Poetry* © 2008 Craig Arnold. "Incubus" from *Made Flesh* © 2008 Craig Arnold. Reprinted by permission of Copper Canyon Press, www.coppercanyonpress.org.

David Barber: "The Threshers" and "The Lather" from *The Spirit Level* © 1995 David Barber. Reprinted by permission of TriQuarterly Books/Northwestern University Press. "Matchbook Hymn," "A Colonial Epitaph Annotated," "Eulogy for an Anchorite," and "Wallenda Sutra" from *Wonder Cabinet* © 2006 David Barber. Reprinted by permission of TriQuarterly Books/Northwestern University Press.

Rick Barot: "The Horses" and "Iowa" are reprinted from *Want* by Rick Barot © 2008 Rick Barot. Reprinted by permission of Sarabande, www.sarabandebooks.org. "Study," "Nearing Rome," "At Point Reyes," "Reading Plato," and "Bonnard's Garden" are reprinted from *The Darker Fall* by Rick Barot © 2002 Rick Barot. Reprinted by permission of Sarabande Books, www.sarabandebooks.org.

Priscilla Becker: "Snowdonia" from *Internal West* © 2001 Priscilla Becker. Reprinted by permission of the author. "Last in Water Series," "New Desert," "Neglect," "Monarch," "Seasonal Poem," and "White Tone" appear courtesy of the author © 2009 Priscilla Becker.

Geoffrey Brock: "And Day Brought Back My Night," "The Beautiful Animal," "Her Voice When She Is Feeling Weak," "The Last Dinner Party," "The Starvers," "Mezzo Cammin," and "Diretto" from *Weighing Light* © 2005 Geoffrey Brock. Reprinted by permission of Ivan R. Dee. "Homeland Security: 2006" and "The Nights" first appeared in *Poetry* © 2008 Geoffrey Brock. "One Morning" first appeared in the *New Criterion* © 2008 Geoffrey Brock.

Daniel Brown: "Missing It," "The Birth of God," "My Own Traces," "Though Angelless," "Prayer," "Something Like That," "'Why Do I Exist?'" and "On Being Asked by Our Receptionist if I Liked the Flowers" from *Taking the Occasion* © 2008 Daniel Brown. Reprinted by permission of Ivan R. Dee. "A Math Grad" first appeared in the *New Criterion* ©

"Warhol's Portraits" first appeared in *Interval(le)s* © 2008 George Green. "Stephen Duck and Edward Chicken" first appeared in *Hanging Loose* © 2001 George Green.

Joseph Harrison: "Nautical Terms" and "To My Friends" from *Identity Theft* © 2008 Joseph Harrison. Reprinted by permission of Waywiser Press. "Variation on a Theme by the Weather," "From the Songbook of Henri Provence," and "The Eccentric Traveler" from *Someone Else's Name* © 2003 Joseph Harrison. Reprinted by permission of Waywiser Press.

Ernest Hilbert: "Domestic Situation," "Magnificent Frigatebird," "Mirage," "Church Street," "Fortunate Ones," and "In Bed for a Week" from *Sixty Sonnets* © 2009 Ernest Hilbert. Reprinted by permission of Red Hen Press. "Ashore" first appeared in the *Yale Review* © 2009 Ernest Hilbert. "Pirates" first appeared in the *New Criterion* © 2007 Ernest Hilbert. "All of You on the Good Earth" first appeared as a limited edition broadside from Temporary Culture Press and appears courtesy of the author © 2008 Ernest Hilbert.

Adam Kirsch: "The tin balls that the Planetarium," "The Consolations," "The long, squat, leaden-windowed, burrow-like," "Calmly, the papers calculate the chance," from *Invasions* © 2008 Adam Kirsch. Reprinted by permission of Ivan R. Dee. "Heroes Have the Whole Earth for Their Tomb" and "A Love Letter" from *The Thousand Wells* © 2002 Adam Kirsch. Reprinted by permission of Ivan R. Dee.

Joanie Mackowski: "Portrait" first appeared in *Del Sol Review* © 2004 Joanie Mackowski. "Larger" first appeared in *Poetry* © 2003 Joanie Mackowski. "Under the Shadow" first appeared in *Yale Review* © 2004 Joanie Mackowski. "Walking in the Dark" first appeared in *Poetry* © 2007 Joanie Mackowski. "View from a Temporary Window" appears courtesy of the author © 2009 Joanie Mackowski.

Eric McHenry: "Rebuilding Year," "Fire Diary," "Point Lobos," "No Daughter," "Figurative North Topeka," and "'Please Please Me'" from *Potscrubber Lullabies* © 2006 Eric McHenry. Reprinted by permission of Waywiser Press.

Molly McQuade: "Synchronized Swimming" first appeared in *Antioch Review* © 2000 Molly McQuade. "Before" first appeared in the *New Criterion* © 2007 Molly McQuade. "Artisan, Expired" first appeared in *Parnassus: Poetry in Review* © Molly McQuade. "Lives of the Jewelers," "Buddhists, Left Hanging," and "Pulse Grass" appear courtesy of the author © 2009 Molly McQuade.

Joshua Mehigan: "Promenade," "Two New Fish," "In the Home of My Sitter," "The Optimist," "Rabbit's Foot," "Merrily," and "Confusing Weather" from *The Optimist* © 2004 Joshua Mehigan. Reprinted by permission of Swallow Press/Ohio University Press. "Father Birmingham" first appeared in *Parnassus: Poetry in Review* © 2008 Joshua Mehigan. "Citation" first appeared in *Poetry* © 2008 Joshua Mehigan. "To Church School" appears courtesy of the author © 2009 Joshua Mehigan.

Wilmer Mills: "Rest Stop, Alabama" first appeared in the *New Republic* © 2001 Wilmer Mills. "The Dowser's Ear," "Rain," and "Morning Song" from *Light for the Orphans* © 2002 Wilmer Mills. Reprinted by permission of the author. "Berkeley Café" appears courtesy of the author.

Joe Osterhaus: "Rainswept" and "The Running of the Blues" from *Radiance* © 2002 Joe Osterhaus. Reprinted by permission of the author. "Food Lion, Winchester, Tennessee" was first published in *Slate*™ *Magazine* (www.slate.com) © 2008 Joe Osterhaus. "The Aughts," "Three-Card Monte," "Next," and "Song" appear courtesy of the author © 2009 Joe Osterhaus.

J. Allyn Rosser: "Street Boy," "Internal Revenue," "Asceticism for Dummies," "Letter to a Young Squirrel," "Subway Seethe," "Aftermath," and "Before You Go" are reprinted from *Foiled Again* by J. Allyn Rosser, © 2007 J. Allyn Rosser. Reprinted by permission of Ivan R. Dee and the author.

A. E. Stallings: "Watching the Vulture at the Road Kill," "A Postcard from Greece," and "Persephone Writes a Letter to Her Mother" from *Archaic Smile* © 1999 A. E. Stallings. reprinted by permission of the University of Evansville Press. "Asphodel," "Aftershocks," and "Fragment" from *Hapax* © 2006 A. E. Stallings. Reprinted by permission of TriQuarterly Books/Northwestern University Press. "Olives" first appeared in the *New Criterion* © 2006 A. E. Stallings. "On Visiting a Borrowed Country House in Arcadia" first appeared in *Poetry* © 2007 A. E. Stallings. "The Catch" first appeared in *Poetry* © 2008 A. E. Stallings. "The Ghost Ship" first appeared in *Smartish Pace* © 2005 A. E. Stallings.

Pimone Triplett: "To My Cousin in Bangkok, Age 16," "Spleen," and "Bird of Paradise Aubade with Bangkok Etching Over the Bed" from *The Price of Light* © 2005 Pimone Triplett. Reprinted by permission of Four Way Books, www.fourwaybooks.com. "First Child Miscarried" and "The Rumor of Necessity" appear courtesy of the author © 2009 Pimone Triplett.

Catherine Tufariello: "Vanishing Twin" first appeared in *The Dark Horse* © 2008 Catherine Tufariello. "Bête Noire" first appeared in *Poetry* © 2007 Catherine Tufariello. "Jigsaw" first appeared in *American Arts Quarterly* © 2009 Catherine Tufariello. "The Escape Artist" first appeared in *The Dark Horse* © 2008 Catherine Tufariello. "Mary Magdalene" from *Annunciations* © 2001 Catherine Tufariello. Reprinted by permission of Aralia Press. "The Mirror" and "Ghost Children" from *Keeping My Name*, winner of the Walt McDonald First-Book Prize in poetry, © 2004 Catherine Tufariello, published by Texas Tech University Press. Reprinted with permission. "S'i' fosse foco, arderei 'l mondo" from *Free Time* © 2001 Catherine Tufariello. Reprinted by permission of Robert L. Barth.

Deborah Warren: "Anna, Emma," "Closing," "Third Person," "Flight," "Regret," "Fire," "A Simple Thing," and "Autumn Afternoon" from *Zero Meridian* © 2004 Deborah Warren. Reprinted with permission of Ivan R. Dee. "Clay and Flame," "Airplane," and "Scope" from *The Size of Happiness* © 2003 Deborah Warren. Reprinted with permission of Waywiser Press.

Rachel Wetzsteon: "Pemberley," "Gusts," "Largo," "Love and Work," "A Pre-Raphaelite Girlhood," "On Leaving the Bachelorette Brunch," "Madeleine for a While," and "Short Ode to Screwball Women" from *Sakura Park* © 2006 Rachel Wetzsteon. Reprinted by permission of Persea Books, Inc. (New York).

Greg Williamson: "Outbound," "*Italics, Mine*," and "The Dial Tone" from *The Silent Partner* ©1995 Greg Williamson. Reprinted by permission of the author. "XIV. Medical

School Skeleton with Dominoes Pizza Man," "XV. Profiles: Anne Dancing with Skeleton," "The Life and Times of Wile E. Coyote, Super Genius," and "Binocular Diplopia" from *Errors in the Script* © 2001 Greg Williamson. Reprinted by permission of The Overlook Press/Peter Mayer Publishers, Inc. "Time" and "Fire" from *A Most Marvelous Piece of Luck* © 2008 Greg Williamson. Reprinted by permission of Waywiser Press.

Christian Wiman: "Hard Night" from *Hard Night* © 2005 Christian Wiman. Reprinted with the permission of Copper Canyon Press, www.coppercanyonpress.org. "Clearing" and "What I Know" from *The Long Home* © 1998 Christian Wiman. Reprinted with the permission of Copper Canyon Press, www.coppercanyonpress.org. "From a Window" first appeared in the *Atlantic* © 2008 Christian Wiman. "Dream of a Dead Friend," "Sitting Down to Breakfast Alone," and "Late Fragment" first appeared in the *New Criterion* © 2009 Christian Wiman.

Mark Wunderlich: "From a Vacant House," "Take Good Care of Yourself," and "Difficult Body" from *The Anchorage* © 1999 Mark Wunderlich. Reprinted by permission of University of Massachusetts Press. "Amaryllis," "Lamb," "Tack," and "The Buck" from *Voluntary Servitude* © 2004 Mark Wunderlich. Reprinted with the permission of Graywolf Press, Saint Paul, Minnesota, www.graywolfpress.org.

David Yezzi: "Free Period" first appeared in *New Ohio Review* © 2009 David Yezzi. "The Call," "The Good News," and "Azores" from *Azores* © 2008 David Yezzi. Reprinted by permission of Swallow Press/Ohio University Press.

C. Dale Young: "Torn," "*Recitativo*," "Sepsis," "Or Something Like That," "In the Cutting Room," "Inheritance," and "The Bridge" appear courtesy of the author © 2009 C. Dale Young.